PRAYERS FOR PILGRIMS

First published in 1993 by
Darton, Longman and Todd Ltd
1 Spencer Court
140–142 Wandsworth High Street
London SW18 4JJ

© 1993 John Johansen-Berg

ISBN 0–232–52046–1

A catalogue record for this book is available
from the British Library

Phototypeset in 10/11pt Ehrhardt by Intype, London
Printed and bound in Great Britain by
Page Bros, Norwich

Contents

To my wife Joan,
a partner in work and
an encourager in the faith
whose love and support have been constant

Acknowledgements

I express my thanks to various friends for their help, especially to Maggie Hamilton whose patient work on the computer, producing revisions and re-drafts, made possible the final version for the publisher.

The biblical quotations for each day are taken from the Holy Bible, New International Version © 1973, 1978, 1984 by the International Bible Society, and used by permission of Hodder and Stoughton Ltd.

Preface

This book of prayers and meditations has been written for individuals and groups to share in daily prayers based on readings from Genesis, Exodus, Acts and Ephesians.

Each day has an opening meditation verse, an introduction from a psalm, a Bible reading and meditation, prayers and a closing benediction. Some of the opening meditations and benedictions are part of a cycle in common with an earlier volume, *Prayers of the Way*. It is envisaged that there will be periods of silence and that there may be music, songs and free prayers as suggested by the worship leader. Though particularly useful for ecumenical groups, the prayers are also suitable for individual meditation and worship. When readings are short it may be helpful to have an additional reading and groups may wish to follow the reading(s) with a short response.

Usually the first prayer follows the theme of the reading. Other prayers may be meditations, intercessions or on such themes as mission, reconciliation and peace. As intercessions often arise from particular circumstances it may be helpful to include specific intercessions between the second and third prayers.

The Prayers for the Day are given in the appendix. These are ancient prayers of the church and a prayer used when lighting a candle for peace. It is suggested that the appropriate prayer follows the Responsorial Psalm each day. The Universal Prayer for Peace, recommended for use each day before the Benediction, is the final prayer in the appendix. Spoken in many languages it unites people of different nations and faiths in a common prayer for peace in our world.

Some of the material was originally written for use in the daily worship of the Community for Reconciliation, an ecumenical Christian community committed to mission, peace and reconciliation. In some weeks we also use the sections of the Affirmation and Pledge to Action of the Community, copies of which are available from Barnes Close, Chadwich, nr Bromsgrove, Worcs. B61 0RA.

In your pilgrimage may you know the peace of God 'who reconciled us to himself through Christ and gave us the ministry of reconciliation'.

JOHN JOHANSEN-BERG

PRAYERS
OF THE PLANET

Readings from Genesis. This is the wonderful story of creation, showing with what loving care God made the world, its animals and people. It speaks with great relevance to our own generation when it is so urgent that we express a proper stewardship in our care of planet earth. The growing sense of our interconnectedness will be encouraged by our understanding of the story of the making of our world.

DAY 1

You are the light of the rising morn
You are the light of the noonday sun
You are the light that scatters the darkness
You are my God, my Saviour and my Lord

RESPONSORIAL PSALM: 148:1–6

L: Praise the Lord.
   Praise the Lord from the heavens, praise him in the heights above.
R: Praise him, all his angels,
   praise him, all his heavenly hosts.

L: Praise him, sun and moon,
   praise him, all you shining stars.
R: Praise him, you highest heavens
   and you waters above the skies.

L: Let them praise the name of the Lord,
   for he commanded and they were created.
R: He set them in place for ever and ever;
   he gave a decree that will never pass away.

READING: Genesis 1:1–5

MEDITATION

The vast universe in primeval darkness,
      creation of God, earth and heaven.
From the chaos came order, from the darkness light.
The light spread gently through the universe,
      darkness fled away.
The light became brighter
      and God saw that it was good, so good.

We take this beautiful creation so much for granted.
What we see with our eyes, what we hear,
      what we smell, what we touch.
All is part of a lovely gift.
Yet we have wasted the earth through our selfish demands.
We need to recover a sense of earth as precious;
      earth as our mother;
as she has nourished us
      so we should care for her with tenderness.

'And there was light.' (1:3)

PRAYERS

Creator God,
   we thank you for the gift of planet earth,
      for the beauty of the day in its brightness,
      for the restfulness by night in the dark.

We confess that we have not been worthy of your gift;
   we have despoiled the earth we inherited;
   we have ignored nature's laws of health;
   we have disobeyed your word.
Forgive us and help us to take better care
   of our common homeland, mother earth.

Blessed Carpenter,
   chisel me into a shape fit for your work;
   plane me into an instrument fit for your kingdom;
   remake me into a vessel fit for your wine
   and reshape me for the glory of your name.

Lord,
   in your creating is my beginning,
   in your speaking is my living,
   in your dying is my saving,
   in your rising is my hoping.

RESPONSE

L: When all seems dark and we feel abandoned in chaos
R: the Lord God brings light; his Spirit restores order and happiness.

May the Lord who brought order from chaos
May the Lord who created the heavens and earth
May the Lord who formed seas and oceans
Guide and uphold you now and always

DAY 2

Lost in the wonder of the Milky Way
Wandering in the vastness of the myriad stars
Journeying to distant planets far from earth
Your people learn more of your greatness,
King of the great Universe

RESPONSORIAL PSALM: 19:1–6

L: The heavens declare the glory of God;
   the skies proclaim the work of his hands.

R: Day after day they pour forth speech;
   night after night they display knowledge.

L: There is no speech or language
   where their voice is not heard.

R: Their voice goes out into all the earth,
   their words to the ends of the world.

L: In the heavens he has pitched a tent for the sun,
   which is like a bridegroom coming forth from his pavilion,
   like a champion rejoicing to run his course.

R: It rises at one end of the heavens
   and makes its circuit to the other;
   nothing is hidden from its heat.

READING: Genesis 1:6–8

MEDITATION

The vastness of the sky,
   ethereal blue by day,
   deepness of black by night,
      handiwork of God.
These are the great spaces of God's creation.

When we meditate,
   looking up at the great expanse of the sky,
we gain some small idea of the grandeur of God.
For we see the signature of God
   in the beauty of his creation.
Let us therefore be concerned about the purity
   of the air we breathe;
when we preserve the quality of the atmosphere
   we encourage our own health and well-being.

'God called the expanse "sky".' (1:8)

PRAYERS

Living God,
   we thank you for the beauty of the sky,
      for great spaces high above us,
      for layered clouds piled high in the heavens,

for the blaze of glory in the sunset,
for the breath of life in pure air.
We confess that we have not treasured your gift;
we have polluted the air through industry;
we have scarred our lungs with smoke;
we have poisoned the atmosphere with radiation.
Forgive us and help us to make more effort
to keep the air pure and to preserve a healthy environment
for the welfare of others and ourselves.

Mother hen, brooding over your chicks,
sister, friend, gathering your family around you,
loving Father, drawing us close to you,
keep us under the shadow of your wings,
enfold us in your love, so deep and strong.

Come, Spirit of God, fill the universe with light
Come, Spirit of God, fill the planet with your love
Come, Spirit of God, fill the church with your joy
Come, Spirit of God, fill the people with your peace.

RESPONSE

L: The sun shines bright in the heavens, symbol of power and love.
*R: Help us to reflect something of your love and power
in lives offered to you in joyful service.*

May the light of the sky give you hope
May the sound of the seas give you inspiration
May the scent of the earth surround you with joy
May the God of all creation bless you through all your days

DAY 3

Refreshing showers moisten the earth
Rushing streams irrigate the desert
Rain, God's blessing for a parched world
Water, the moisture of life, for thirsty people

RESPONSORIAL PSALM: 93

L: The Lord reigns, he is robed in majesty;
    the Lord is robed in majesty
    and is armed with strength.

R: The world is firmly established;
    it cannot be moved.

L: Your throne was established long ago;
    you are from all eternity.

R: The seas have lifted up, O Lord,
    the seas have lifted up their voice;
    the seas have lifted up their pounding waves.

L: Mightier than the thunder of the great waters,
    mightier than the breakers of the sea—
    the Lord on high is mighty.

R: Your statutes stand firm;
    holiness adorns your house for endless days, O Lord.

READING: Genesis 1:9–10

MEDITATION

The sea, wide and deep;
    the sea, holding its mystery;
        the sea, vast in its beauty;
this is the creation of God.

When I stand on the deck of a ship
    and look out over the tumultuous waves,
    across the expanse of foaming ocean,
I am conscious of another world,
    of all that lives in the sea;
strange and beautiful creatures
    moving silently in a world of luminous colour;
great whales, shellfish, shy, playful dolphins,
    shoals of silver fish darting through rock crevices.
We can preserve the beauty of this vast underwater universe
    or we can destroy it with poisons,
    killing whole species to cut costs in a factory.
May God give us the grace to treasure the seas.

'The gathered waters he called "seas".' (1:10)

PRAYERS

Holy God,
 we thank you for the wide expanse of the sea,
  for the deep mysteries of the oceans,
  for the teeming life in rivers and lakes,
  for the benefit of pure water to drink.
 We confess that we have not appreciated this gift as we should;
  we have allowed industrial waste to pour into rivers;
  we have polluted lakes with impurities;
  we have made the seas dumping grounds for nuclear waste;
  we have allowed many people to die
   for lack of pure water to drink.
 Forgive us and help us to recognise that water is life,
  to preserve the purity of streams and rivers,
  to take proper care of the seas and oceans,
  to make a common effort to provide wells of pure water
   for all those who lack them.

Make our feet walk in your way, Lord;
make our voice speak your word, Lord;
make our hands serve you in blessing others;
may our lives show something of your glory.

In the movement of clouds, stars and planets
 we see your moving hand, Lord God.
In the movement of rivers, lakes and oceans
 we see your moving hand, Lord God.
In the movement of heart, blood and foetus
 we see your moving hand, Lord God.
In the movement of soul from earth to eternity
 we see your moving hand, Lord God.

RESPONSE

L: Father, in times of spiritual drought,
   when we thirst for righteousness
*R: you give us the living water
  and lead us beside flowing streams.*

May the showers of God's blessing fall upon you
May the streams of Christ's love refresh you
May the rivers of the Spirit uphold you
May the blessed Trinity fill you with joy and peace

<table>
<tr><td>

DAY
4

</td><td>

Granite, hard crag-face, lasting through ages
Sandstone, soft, worn away by the weather of the years
Marble, beautiful, veined, ready for artistic shaping
Rocks of time, formed by the creative wisdom,
*   give praise to God, architect of the universe*

</td></tr>
</table>

RESPONSORIAL PSALM: 95:1–5

    L: Come, let us sing for joy to the Lord;
          let us shout aloud to the Rock of our salvation.
    R: Let us come before him with thanksgiving
         and extol him with music and song.

    L: For the Lord is the great God,
          the great King above all gods.
    R: In his hand are the depths of the earth,
         and the mountain peaks belong to him.

    L: The sea is his, for he made it,
    R: and his hands formed the dry land.

READING: Genesis 1:11–13

MEDITATION

    Earth, warm and brown; our planet earth
        producing the seed, the plant, the fruit,
           a gift of God;
        productive earth, so beautiful.
    And God saw that it was very good.

    And people saw that it was good too.
    People also saw that crops can create wealth
        and that minerals under the earth can yield riches.
    So the earth is scarred by human greed;
        the fields are made to maximise their yield;
        deep mines are sunk
           to give up the gold and diamonds formed through millennia;
        vast rain forests are felled to make a few people rich.
    So our tears fall for mother earth
        who has been so ravaged by those who should protect her,
          treasure her for her beauty
          and appreciate the natural loveliness
            she displays season by season.

'*The land produced vegetation.*' (1:12)

PRAYERS

    Loving God,
        we thank you for our joy in mother earth;
           for her fruitfulness in the crops of field and orchard;

for the hidden seeds giving the promise of harvest;
for the colours, scents and sounds of beautiful nature.
We confess that we have not been worthy of such gifts;
we have plundered the earth for its riches;
we have greedily exhausted the earth in our sowing;
we have not shared the harvests fairly among people.
Forgive us and help us to care more lovingly for mother earth;
as she has provided so bountifully for us,
so may we find joy in providing abundantly for others;
help us to realise that we are bonded together
with all your children and are called to live in harmony
on this beautiful planet earth.

I offer my love to you, Lord,
and accept your joy from you;
I offer my joy to you, Lord,
and accept your peace from you;
I offer my peace to you, Lord,
and accept your love from you.

Seedtime and harvest, gift of the Lord of the sun
Harvest of lakes and seas, gift of the Lord of the rain
Harvest of field and mine, gift of the Lord of the earth
Seedtime and harvest, gift of the Lord of the seasons

THE LORD'S PRAYER

RESPONSE
L: Lord, you have given us mother earth,
rich in productive gifts for the benefit of all.
R: Help us to treasure her,
and to care for her health and welfare.

As the fields are green with the coming of spring
As the trees are clothed afresh with abundance of leaves
As the plants push through the earth's crust with new life
So may God grant you a new springtime of faith

<table>
<tr><td>

DAY
5

</td><td>

God of the shining stars, smile on me
God of the laughing moon, laugh with me
God of the burning sun, set me on fire
Great God of the planets, be my guide

</td></tr>
</table>

RESPONSORIAL PSALM: 136:1, 4–9

L: Give thanks to the Lord, for he is good.
R: His love endures for ever.

L: to him who alone does great wonders,
  his love endures for ever.
R: who by his understanding made the heavens,
  his love endures for ever.

L: who spread out the earth upon the waters,
  his love endures for ever.
R: who made the great lights—
  his love endures for ever.

L: the sun to govern the day,
  his love endures for ever.
R: the moon and stars to govern the night;
  his love endures for ever.

READING: Genesis 1:14–19

MEDITATION

The beauty of the shining lights, sun and moon;
  the sun to be the light by day,
  the moon to be the light by night.
Overcoming the darkness, encouraging natural growth,
  illuminating our path.

When in the night I look up at the night sky
  and see the bright lights of the Great Bear,
    the splendour of the Milky Way
    or the distinctive brightness of a new star,
  I am filled with a sense of peace,
  knowing that the God who created
    this vast universe of beauty,
  who fashioned unknown planets
    in their undiscovered loveliness,
  also created us and knows us,
    holds us in the hollow of his hand
    and yearns that we have health and well-being
    and that in deep communion with him
      we should find our peace.

'He also made the stars.' (1:16)

10

PRAYERS

Wise and loving Creator,
we give you praise and thanks for the light of our eyes,
for the burning sun at noon,
for the softness of moonlight at midnight,
for the glimmering of stars in a dark velvet sky,
for the glorious riot of colour at sunset
and the golden glory of the dawn.
We confess that we too often take all this for granted
and fail to recognise the great privilege that is ours
in the gift of light.
Keep us ever mindful of your love.
May we express our thanksgiving
in lives offered in your service.

Lord,
hold our life in yours.
Lead us in your way,
not by our desires but by your will,
not by our weakness but by your strength.
May our pilgrimage find fulfilment
in your presence, for your glory.

Lord of the leaf, God of the stars,
Giver of water, Creator of oceans,
Father of mercy, Saviour of love,
Spirit of peace, holy Three,
abide with us always.

RESPONSE

L: Lord God, when we look up at the sky at night,
when we see the stars in abundance and the light of the moon,
R: help us to know your peace in our hearts
and to experience your light in our lives.

As the sun in its shining brings glory
As the stars in the night scatter dark
As the moon gives us hope in its radiance
So may the light of God
fill your heart and your mind and your life

<table>
<tr><td>

DAY
6

</td><td>

Creatures of the ocean depths, hiding low
Fish of the great lakes, swimming deep
Animals of the wide seas, roving far
Fishing boats and ocean liners traversing the waters
Great God of the seas and rivers
keep you in your journeys by land and sea

</td></tr>
</table>

RESPONSORIAL PSALM: 148:7–12

> L: Praise the Lord from the earth,
>   you great sea creatures and all ocean depths,
> *R: lightning and hail, snow and clouds,*
>   *stormy winds that do his bidding,*
>
> L: you mountains and all hills,
>   fruit trees and all cedars,
> *R: wild animals and all cattle,*
>   *small creatures and flying birds,*
>
> L: kings of the earth and all nations,
>   you princes and all rulers on earth,
> *R: young men and maidens,*
>   *old men and children.*

READING: Genesis 1:20–25

MEDITATION

> What variety and beauty there is
>   in all the creatures of the sea,
>   in all the birds of the skies,
>   in all the animals of the fields.
> It is a lovely world hiding in the woods,
>   of beautiful insects, crawling under the bark of trees,
>   of rainbow fish in streams,
>   of swooping birds whose fine songs
>   fill a valley with nature's praise.
> What a gift! What a beautiful gift
>   to be given the care of such created beings.
>
> Yet so many of them have been trapped,
>   muzzled, penned, mutilated.
> Humankind have so often proved most unkind
>   to the creatures God has committed to our compassion.
> May God forgive us
>   and reconcile us to our animal brothers and sisters.

' *"Let the land produce living creatures".*' (1:24)

PRAYERS

Divine Creator,
we thank you for the sheer delight
of all the beautiful creatures you have made
and placed here to share this planet with us.
For all that swims in the depths of the sea,
for all that flies in the heights of the heavens,
for all that roams in the fields and plains.
We confess that we have not been good stewards.
We have hunted, baited, trapped, tortured and killed
countless numbers of animals, wild and tame.
We have caused the extinction of whole species
by our greed and selfish exploitation of animals.
We have caused sorrow in heaven and grief on earth
by our abuse of birds, beasts and fish.
Forgive us and inspire us to be better stewards.

In the sands of the desert
the water of life is so precious, so needed.
In remote and poverty-shackled villages
the rice of life is so precious, so needed.
In the run-down farms of underdeveloped countries
fertiliser is so precious, so needed.
Yet water is poured out in plenty on lawns of leisure;
rice is thrown into the waste bins of hotels of affluence;
fertiliser is spread plentifully on the golf courses of the wealthy.
God of the poor,
challenge the Zaccheus in each of us,
inspire us to give from our abundance,
to share the good things that have been committed to us,
so that the desert may blossom like the rose
and villages resound with songs of celebration.

Creator King,
you are the living water,
you are the vibrant air,
you are the fruitful earth,
you are the heart of the universe.
Creator, creating, create in me a new spirit
that I may be one with water, air and earth.

RESPONSE

L: Creator of the world, you made the birds of the air
in all their variety and loveliness;
R: you made the fish of the sea and the beasts of the field.
We praise you for the abundance of your living creation.

May the maker of the yellow beak, the black bird, be with you
May the maker of the broad wing, the brown thrush, be with you
May the maker of the fan tail, the white dove, be near you
May the great bird of the wide skies descend upon you

DAY 7

Father, I give you my childhood, for you made me
Shepherd, I give you my middle years, for you sustain me
Lord, I give you the evening of my life, for you keep me
From birth to death, you are my Redeemer

RESPONSORIAL PSALM: 8:3–8

L: When I consider your heavens, the work of your fingers,
   the moon and the stars, which you have set in place,
R: what is man that you are mindful of him,
   the son of man that you care for him?

L: You made him a little lower than the heavenly beings
   and crowned him with glory and honour.
R: You made him ruler over the works of your hands;
   you put everything under his feet:

L: all flocks and herds, and the beasts of the field,
R: the birds of the air, and the fish of the sea,
   all that swim the paths of the seas.

READING: Genesis 1:26–28a

MEDITATION

The Lord God had a desire for fellowship
   so he created man.
He created him to be like himself,
   both male and female in attributes,
   related together in creation for re-creation,
   to bring into the world the fruit of relationship,
   increasing in number, women and men,
   placed in the world to worship God
      and to please him.

What a sublime destiny! to be made like God.
What a sublime challenge! to live up to the image
   in which we are created.
What a sublime hope! that one day the *imago dei*
   will be seen in us by the grace of Christ our Redeemer.

'So God created man in his own image.' (1:27)

PRAYERS

Dear Father,
   in your great love you have created a family
      to share all the delights of the world you made.
   Your children are of such a wonderful variety,
      black, white and yellow; young and old; women and men;
      of many races, speaking varied tongues.

14

We give you thanks that we can learn so much
    from all those around us;
we thank you for our different cultures;
we rejoice in the music, art and poetry
    that is distinctive in each nation.
We rejoice that you have not made us the same
    but beautifully different, yet having so much in common.
We confess that we have not appreciated each other as we ought
    nor accepted each other as we should.
We have marred our world with discrimination;
we have scarred our society with racism and nationalism;
we have made our differences cause for persecution.
Forgive us and help us to care for one another,
    to seek justice and peace for all
    and to respect the integrity of this creation
        of which we are all part,
    being one family, looking to you,
        Creator and Father of all of us.

In the silence I hear you speaking
In the quiet I know your being
Being silent I can hear others
In the stillness we enter deep communion
When words cease and noise abates
    in the silence is my renewing,
    in the quiet is my abiding in you, Lord God.

In the primal time, creation; you made the universe.
In the beginning, creation; you separated earth and sea.
At the outset, creation; you created light in darkness.
In the primal time, creation; you made man and woman in your image.

RESPONSE

L: Holy Father, we thank you for the variety of all your people.
R: Help us to care for one another, rejoicing in our unity and variety.

May the Lord whose birds soar in the skies
May the Lord whose fish abound in the seas
May the Lord whose animals roam the plains
May the Lord whose children people the earth
Bless you abundantly through all your days

DAY 8

Ears of wheat, ripening in the midday sun
Growing barley, refreshed by a shower of rain
Fields of oats, food for animals and people
The blessings of mother earth, given by our God

RESPONSORIAL PSALM: 145:8–13a

L: The Lord is gracious and compassionate,
 slow to anger and rich in love.

R: The Lord is good to all;
 he has compassion on all he has made.

L: All you have made will praise you, O Lord;
 your saints will extol you.

R: They will tell of the glory of your kingdom
 and speak of your might,

L: so that all men may know of your mighty acts
 and the glorious splendour of your kingdom.

R: Your kingdom is an everlasting kingdom,
 and your dominion endures through all generations.

READING: Genesis 1:28b–31

MEDITATION

God gave into the care of humankind
 all the other species he had created in such beauty;
 the abounding fish of rivers, lakes and seas;
 the multifarious birds of woodland, forest and plains;
 the wild and tame animals of field, moorland and jungle.
All this living abounding creation he gave to people
 in a stewardship of trust.
And God looked out over the whole scene
 and he was filled with joy for it was all very good.

But sadly it has not remained so.
 Elephants are brutalised and killed for ivory;
 whales are hunted and slaughtered for profit;
 tigers become trophies for cocktail conversation
 and monkeys are caged for entertainment.
The eagle and the hawk become victims
 of humans' greed and pride;
 whole species have been obliterated
 to satisfy the selfish desires of people.
Across God's creation the cry of the hunted deer is heard;
 to the Creator is lifted up a loud lamentation
 for we human beings have forsaken our stewardship
 and betrayed our Creator.

'Then God said, "I give you every seed-bearing plant on the face of the whole earth".' (1:29)

16

PRAYERS

Divine Weaver,
  you have made a world of intricate beauty
    and related us to each other in your pattern of creation,
    nature, people, animals, earth, sun, stars, rivers, seas,
    woven into one whole yet so varied in individuality.
  We confess that we have not respected
    the ways in which we are interconnected;
      we have torn the fabric of our society;
      we have rent the cloth of our unity;
      we have pulled apart the threads that bind us.
  Forgive us and enable us to remake the pattern,
    to restore all that binds us,
    people to people, animals and people,
    humankind to earth, your children to you,
  so that we may be again what you intended us to be,
    unique in our individuality
      yet whole and together in our interconnected world.

I searched for you in philosophies and books,
I searched for you in theories and creeds,
  but you eluded me.
I searched for you in libraries and museums,
I searched for you in cathedrals and churches,
  but you eluded me.
I searched for you in banks and building societies,
I searched for you in factories and showrooms,
  but you eluded me.
I searched for you amongst the poor and broken of the haciendas,
I searched for you amongst the weak and despised of the refugee camps,
  and you welcomed me;
and then I found you in all the other places
  as I joined with others to express your compassion.

God of the thunderclap, your power surrounds us
God of the earthquake, your energy astounds us
God of the raging fire, your glory blinds us
God of the gentle breeze, your love finds us

RESPONSE

L: Creator God, you have given us care of all the living creatures.
R: Help us to care for all animals, wild or tame.

May God who made male and female bless you
May God who gave dominion over all living creatures guide you
May God who promised you the products of the earth
  grant you good harvests
May God who made everything good bless you with abundance

<table>
<tr><td>

DAY
9

</td><td>

The oak grows strong, broad leaves and green
The poplar reaches high, slim leaves shining
The yew, thick, low, leaves ever-green
The willow, drooping by the lake, leaves delicate and long
The trees too are in your care, Lord of creation

</td></tr>
</table>

RESPONSORIAL PSALM: 32:1–2, 5–7

L: Blessed is he whose transgressions are forgiven,
     whose sins are covered.

R: Blessed is the man whose sin the Lord does not count against him
*   and in whose spirit is no deceit.*

L: Then I acknowledged my sin to you
     and did not cover up my iniquity.

R: I said 'I will confess my transgressions to the Lord'–
*   and you forgave the guilt of my sin.*

L: Therefore let everyone who is godly pray to you
     while you may be found;

R: surely when the mighty waters rise,
*   they will not reach him.*

L: You are my hiding place;
     you will protect me from trouble

R: and surround me with songs of deliverance.

READING: Genesis 2:8–9, 15–17

MEDITATION

This is how God intended people to live–
   in the beauty of a garden,
      surrounded by trees, each bearing fruit in season,
      all their needs met in the productivity of mother earth,
      finding happiness in obedience to their Creator.

When I stand in a well-kept garden and survey the scene
   I am on the edge of paradise.
Smooth lawns of green grass are a carpet to the feet;
   a thousand flowers bloom in beds and rockeries;
   the trees give promise of luscious fruit;
   butterflies and bees add colour and sound;
   the fountains sparkle as refreshing water arches high
      and falls with music back into the pool.
Here is a reminder of Eden,
   God's gift to his people, created in his image.
Here is beauty that no painter can capture,
   loveliness that no sculptor can hope to imitate.
In such a garden God spoke to humankind;
   he asked of us obedience in matters of good and evil;
God placed us in a beautiful garden

and pleaded with us to choose the light,
to choose life.

' *"You must not eat from the tree of the knowledge of good and evil."* ' (2:17)

PRAYERS

Lord of the vineyard,
we give you thanks for the loveliness of gardens,
for the beauty of flower and blossom,
for the delight of fruits and berries,
for the refreshing fountains and ponds,
for the glory of the green of nature,
for the riot of colour in cultivated beds,
for the cheerful songs of carefree birds,
for the barking of playful dogs
and for the laughter of children.
Forgive us that so often we fail in gratitude
for gifts so great and varied.
Help us to rejoice in all the sights and sounds
that surround us in nature
and to share with others the good things
we receive from you.

See in the universe your tears, dear Lord,
weeping with the fallen citizens of Jerusalem,
crying with the oppressed slaves in Rome,
weeping for the tortured martyrs of an empire,
crying for the child victims of a barbarian horde.
See in the universe your tears, dear Lord,
weeping for black people oppressed by a white civilisation,
crying for the families of the disappeared,
weeping for those persecuted by communist domination,
crying for the children in the camps of the Palestinian people.
We see in the universe your tears, Lord,
mingling with the tears of those for whom you died.

In the one is singleness, blessed unity.
In the three is community, holy trinity.
In the seven is completeness, all created.
Gift of the Three in One is full salvation;
come quickly, Lord, Saviour and Redeemer.

RESPONSE

L: Lord, you created a world of beauty; you gave us paradise.
*R: Forgive us for our failure to respond to your love with love;
forgive us for despoiling the face of your creation.*

May the Father walk with you in the cool of the garden
May the Son walk with you on the mountain path
May the Spirit walk with you in the pilgrim way
The blessing of Father, Son and Spirit be on you always

DAY 10

Raindrops falling from the sky, as the tears of God
Sun shining brightly in the heavens, as the smile of God
Rainbow in the sky, sun and rain, as the promise of God
For God is with us both in sorrow and in joy

RESPONSORIAL PSALM: 51:1–3, 10–12

    L: Have mercy on me, O God, according to your unfailing love;
    R: according to your great compassion blot out my transgressions.

    L: Wash away all my iniquity
        and cleanse me from my sin.
    R: For I know my transgressions,
        and my sin is always before me.

    L: Create in me a pure heart, O God,
        and renew a steadfast spirit within me.
    R: Do not cast me from your presence
        or take your Holy Spirit from me.

    L: Restore to me the joy of your salvation
    R: and grant me a willing spirit, to sustain me.

READING: Genesis 3:1–8

MEDITATION

    If we listen we can hear the voice of God;
    but in a world of good and evil
        there will always be a tempter's voice.
    The guile of the serpent
        suggests that there is some experience we lack,
            some power that we need, some goods that we must own,
            some knowledge that we must have,
        and nothing must stand in the way of attaining it,
            neither love of God nor love of neighbour.
    When we listen to the voice of temptation,
        when we act upon it to satisfy our selfish desires,
    then we are afraid to meet with God
        and we do not want to hear his voice.
    We have fallen from the state of grace;
        we have gone out from the garden of delight;
        we see ourselves in the ugliness of disobedience.
    When shall we regain the innocence of the garden of Eden?
    When shall we be pleasing to God and delight to walk with him?
    By the grace of God, Christ will lead us
        to that promised garden;
    he will restore us as children to our Father
        and his chosen costly way is through the garden of Gethsemane
            and the tree of Calvary.

'They hid from the Lord God.' (3:8)

PRAYERS

Loving Shepherd,
   you care for us even when we are unaware of you;
   you warn us of dangers, snares and temptations;
   you long for us to be safe in the fold.
Yet we desire to go our own way;
   our pride makes us think we know better than you;
   we disobey your loving direction;
   we stray from the path of safety and righteousness
      and wander into danger and evil ways.
Guide us gently back into the fold of your keeping
   where we are known and loved, individually and together.
So may we find joy and peace in your presence
   and live to the glory of God our Father.

Lord,
   it sometimes seems that I have passed this way before
      in my circular journey of pilgrimage,
   when I confirm my commitment to you
      and promise you my life, my wealth, my years.
   It sometimes seems that I have passed this way before
      when I confess my failures
         and recognise my half-heartedness and broken promises.
   It sometimes seems that I have passed this way before
      when I express faith that is firm and hope that is bright
      and offer my life for your service to the end of time.
Lord, help me to break out of the circle
   and spiral upwards, journeying with your Spirit.
Bring me to the place of meeting
   that I might be confirmed in discipleship
   and made ready to serve you faithfully.

When the wanderer returns to you, Lord God, there is joy
When the lost sheep is found, there is joy
When the lost son comes home, there is joy
Give us joy in our fellowship
   and peace in your presence, God of the pilgrim way.

RESPONSE

L: When we are tempted to doubt or despair,
      when we are tempted to pride, envy or greed,
*R: may we recall the life and teaching of our Lord
      and overcome temptation in our renewed dedication to him.*

*May the Lord of the running deer be alongside you
May the Lord of the living water journey with you
May the Lord of the flying crane be your guide
May the Lord of the flowing air go with you*

PRAYERS
OF LIBERATION

Readings from Exodus. This is a dramatic story of the liberation of God's people from slavery. It is written in a particular context but speaks powerfully to our own generation, especially to oppressed and deprived people. In many places people have journeyed through the wilderness towards the promised land. They will find great encouragement in this account of God's faithfulness to his people. It will encourage all who realise that each of us needs to take a journey of liberation in our spiritual pilgrimage.
Some of the other prayers are based on verses from 1 John.

DAY 11

The darkness when the light of sun and moon is withdrawn
Darkness when not even the glimmer of stars brightens the sky
Darkness when standing alone you can see nothing
Yet God is there in the darkness too;
with him the night is as bright as day

RESPONSORIAL PSALM: 119:1–2, 5–6

L: Blessed are they whose ways are blameless,
   who walk according to the law of the Lord.
R: Blessed are they who keep his statutes
   and seek him with all their heart.

L: Oh, that my ways were steadfast in obeying your decrees!
R: Then I would not be put to shame
   when I consider all your commands.

AFFIRMATION AND PLEDGE: Section 1

READING: Exodus 1:8–14

MEDITATION

It is always the error of oppressors that they think they can gain more from people by rough treatment and hard labour. For years the Israelites served happily in Egypt, a mutual respect producing a creative partnership. But envy and fear produced a bitter oppression. The Pharaoh was in a position of absolute power; such power often corrupts and its selfish use brings suffering to many people. We have seen it in many generations with the rise and fall of innumerable dictators.

There in Egypt the chosen people suffered bitter treatment, used as slave labour to produce great buildings for the increased prestige of a great empire. The days of gratitude to Joseph and his family had given way to fear of the growing tribe of immigrants. This was the beginning of the great sufferings of the Israelites in Egypt.

'They made their lives bitter with hard labour.' (1:14)

PRAYERS

God of Abraham and Moses,
   you are with your people
      when the way is through pleasant valleys
      and in a country of milk and honey,
      with settled villages and happy towns.
   You are with your people
      when the way is through rough pastures,
         in slave camps and the killing fields.
   You are ready to challenge your people in times of ease
      and to comfort your people in times of oppression.

Lord God,
  bring freedom for your people.
  We pray for those who have endured
    long years of political oppression;
      people without a vote, lacking representation,
        treated as flotsam and jetsam
          by those who wield political power.
Lord God,
  bring freedom for your people.
  May there be a silent revolution
    as the aspirations of the people
      become present reality for political masters.
  May those who hold power without responsibility
    yield it to those who hold power by representation.
Lord God,
  bring freedom to your people.

Compassionate Shepherd,
  through you we have the word of life,
    for you have made manifest eternal life
    and you have brought us into fellowship
      with your Father and with you
        and with all your people.
  What was heard with human ears,
  what was seen with human eyes,
  what was touched with human hands
    we proclaim to all around us
      and the good news fills us with joy.

THE LORD'S PRAYER

RESPONSE
  L: Lord, when we face the bitterness of oppression or the night of despair
  R: help us to put our trust in you.

  Your love leads you into the heart of God
  Your trust leads you into the light of God
  Your faith leads you into the place of God
  May you find your centre in the life of God

<table>
<tr><td>

DAY
12

</td><td>

Where the breeze blows softly over spring flowers
Where the wind blows strongly over marsh reeds
Where the gale sweeps fiercely over swaying trees
Know that the God of wind and wave speaks to his people

</td></tr>
</table>

RESPONSORIAL PSALM: 119:9–11, 15–16

> L: How can a young man keep his way pure?
> *R: By living according to your word.*
>
> L: I seek you with all my heart;
>   do not let me stray from your commands.
> *R: I have hidden your word in my heart*
>   *that I might not sin against you.*
>
> L: I meditate on your precepts and consider your ways.
> *R: I delight in your decrees; I will not neglect your word.*

AFFIRMATION AND PLEDGE: Section 2

READING: Exodus 2:1–10

MEDITATION

Each nation that needs a revolution also needs a liberator. In the case of Israel God chose the leader to liberate his people and his plan is seen in the birth and upbringing of Moses. Nothing can frustrate the divine purpose, so what appears tragedy may be the future hope of the people. Hidden in the rushes in a time of oppression was the liberator of Israel; the grief of his mother was turned into joy when she was able to nurse her child growing up in a royal court. All the skills of Egypt were to play their part in preparing a child born for high endeavour. In each generation we should trust God for the way of liberation.

'She named him Moses, saying, "I drew him out of the water." ' (2:10)

PRAYERS

Holy God,
   yours is the kingdom and the glory.
In wisdom you work out your purposes.
   For every person you have your plan;
   for every family your intentions;
   for every nation your calling.
We are often unready to hear your call
   and lazy in fulfilling your purpose.
Yet we are moved to see
   how you make your plan for us before we are born
      and call us for special tasks from childhood to old age.
Make us ever mindful of your presence and your power.

Giver of all good,
   release your people

from the oppression that comes from selfish use of wealth,
from the power of those who control the economy,
from multinational companies with no regard for the poor.
Release your people, Lord.
May there be peaceful but radical change;
may those with economic power recognise their responsibility;
may there be an acceptance of good stewardship
as those who have received good things
become ready to share them with others.
Good Lord, release your people to give and to receive.

Crucified Saviour,
we have a message to proclaim,
that God is light.
We cannot claim fellowship with you
and continue to walk in darkness.
Since by the shedding of your blood
you have taken away our sin,
help us to walk in the light.
We know that we have fallen short;
that we have missed the mark.
Forgive us our wrongdoing
and cleanse us from unrighteousness,
for we ask it in your precious name.

RESPONSE

L: Holy God, you are the Lord of eternity;
R: *you work out your divine purpose in history.*

May the night bring you refreshment of sleep
May the day bring you challenge in work
May your companions bring you the joy of friendship
May God give you peace in your heart

DAY 13

The seed is in the earth, surrounded by warmth and food
The seed grows secretly, day by day
The seed grows purposefully, ready to break through the soil
May the secret seed of your love ever grow within me

RESPONSORIAL PSALM: 119:17–18, 23–24

L: Do good to your servant, and I will live;
　　　I will obey your word.
R: Open my eyes that I may see wonderful things in your law.

L: Though princes sit together and slander me,
　　　your servant will meditate on your decrees.
R: Your statutes are my delight;
　　　they are my counsellors.

AFFIRMATION AND PLEDGE: Section 3

READING: Exodus 2:11–25

MEDITATION

　　　Helping people does not always gain appreciation; the liberator is not always welcomed with open arms. Strong leadership exacts its price as well as giving support. To criticise or attack the Egyptians was one thing but when Moses sought to give guidance to a fellow Israelite he encountered hostility.

　　　Generations do not change the general picture; there are always collaborators; there are always those ready to betray the leaders of their own people. Selfishness knows no national boundaries and it remains true in many places that self-sacrifice is not accepted for the common good. The liberator will face as much of a challenge from his own people as from the oppressors.

' *"Who made you ruler and judge over us?"* ' (2:14)

PRAYERS

Father,
　　　it is not easy when friends betray us;
　　　　　it is hard to understand when a relative denies our calling.
　　　Yet betrayal and denials
　　　　　are part of the story of the human family.
　　　Keep us ever mindful
　　　　　that though our closest friends may betray us
　　　　　　you will never leave us, nor forsake us.
　　　Your love is constant
　　　　　through all the changing circumstances of life.
　　　In you we place our trust.

Loving Shepherd,
　　　we commend to your care your flock,
　　　　　worried and harried by wolves,
　　　　　　prey to thieves and cruel attackers.

Release your sheep from hands
   that seek to do them harm.
Loving Shepherd,
   in many lands your people suffer
      because they uphold the honour of your name.
   They are persecuted and killed
      because they hold the faith with courage.
   Change the minds and hearts of the persecutors
      and release your people from the cruel enmity.
   In every land may each be free
      to worship you and to proclaim your gospel.

Righteous Mediator,
   you are our advocate with the Father.
   By your sacrifice our sins are forgiven,
      for your grace is sufficient
         to take away the sins of the whole world.
   Help us to know the truth;
   help us to obey your commands;
   help us to walk in your way
      so that we may abide in you and you in us.

RESPONSE

L: Lord, you call your people in every generation;
R: help us to be faithful in responding to your call.

Go into a world of need to speak a word of hope
Go into a world of hunger to respond with acts of love
Go into a world of thirst to offer Christ's cup of water
Live and give in the name of the Father, the Son and the Spirit

I close my lips and silent hear your word
I close my eyes and blind I see your face
I close my hands and turn to you in prayer
I open my palms and receive your benediction

RESPONSORIAL PSALM: 119:25–26, 31–32

L: I am laid low in the dust;
     renew my life according to your word.
R: I recounted my ways and you answered me;
     teach me your decrees.

L: I hold fast to your statutes, O Lord;
     do not let me be put to shame.
R: I run in the path of your commands,
     for you have set my heart free.

AFFIRMATION AND PLEDGE: Section 4

READING: Exodus 3:1–12

MEDITATION

   The glory of God was seen on the mountain; the voice of God was heard by his
chosen leaders. In the holiness of that encounter comes the knowledge that God
is the God of the oppressed, of the poor, of the persecuted. He sees their plight
and he appoints his chosen to lead them into freedom. And when the liberator
points to the power of the oppressor and the impossibility of the task, then God
reminds him that the task is not limited by the wisdom, skill or strength of the
liberator but enabled by the presence of God who journeys with him.

   It is no different for us. When the tasks seem impossible then God reminds us
that with him all is possible. By his grace we transcend our own limitations in
working out the divine purpose. And when we are called to give encouragement
to the oppressed and hope to the persecuted we shall receive that calling in an
encounter of great splendour, filled with awe at the voice of God.

' *"I have come down to rescue them from the hand of the Egyptians".*' (3:8)

PRAYERS

   Dearest Lord,
      you grant us precious moments
         when we encounter you in your divine splendour.
      You give us a glimpse of your glory on the mountain top.
      We hear the sound of your voice in the depths of the forest.
      In the heart of prayers in the church
         we bow down with others to acclaim you,
            holy, holy, holy; full of grace and truth.
      So we join in the eternal harmony of songs of praise
         and await your divine command,
            ready to go where you send us.

Lord of good life,
we pray for those who,
seeking their happiness in this world's pleasures
have become enslaved by alcohol.
Unable to take such drink in moderation
their lives become a cycle of despair and drunkenness.
Though they may wish to break free
they find themselves unable to do so.
Lord, help them to find the strength
to make a new beginning
and to find the good life
in your word, your kingdom, your presence
and to enjoy in moderation
those gifts of this world's goods
that you grant them.

Dearest Brother,
we thank you that you have given us a new commandment
– to love one another.
How can we claim to walk with you
yet hate our brother or our sister?
Inspire us with love for our neighbours everywhere
that we may walk in the light
and be an encouragement to others.

RESPONSE
L: Loving Shepherd, your people suffer persecution in many places;
R: may they know that they are surrounded and upheld by many prayers.

Where there is truth, there is God's blessing of peace
Where there is justice, there is God's blessing of peace
Where there is righteousness, there is God's blessing of peace
May the peace of God be in your family, in your nation and in your heart

DAY 15

As the blossom to the fruit
As the seed to the flower
As the acorn to the oak tree
So is my Lord's calling to my discipleship

RESPONSORIAL PSALM: 119:33–34, 36–37

L: Teach me, O Lord, to follow your decrees;
    then I will keep them to the end.
R: Give me understanding, and I will keep your law
    and obey it with all my heart.

L: Turn my heart towards your statutes
    and not towards selfish gain.
R: Turn my eyes away from worthless things;
    renew my life according to your word.

AFFIRMATION AND PLEDGE: Section 5

READING: Exodus 3:13–22

MEDITATION

The oppressor does not readily relax his grip. He will not easily forgo the privileges and advantages he has gained. But God works out his purposes in his sure way; signs and wonders impress and alarm. Those who see something of the mighty word of God are filled with awe. The good man is always ready to co-operate with God. The oppressor who has some wisdom knows when to let go; only the obdurate and stupid continue to defy God and so work for their own destruction. Mere human beings cannot withstand his power nor frustrate his purpose. There is no oppression in today's world so great or terrible but God can overcome it.

' *"I will stretch out my hand and strike the Egyptians with all the wonders that I will perform among them. After that, he will let you go." '* (3:20)

PRAYERS

Lord,
    let me be ready to see your signs;
        the warning signs that call nations to repentance and new paths;
            the signs of grace, rainbows in the sky,
                that assure us of a happy future;
            the travelling signs that indicate
                where we should go and when we should stay.
    Grant us the wisdom to read your signs for our time.

Free those people, Lord,
    enslaved by powder and needle,
    from drugs with all their deadly effects.
Free those people, Lord,
    from the degradation that enslaves,

from the addiction that undermines.
Turn them from reliance on drugs
    to trust in the living God.
Turn them from heroin and opium
    to the fruit of the Spirit.
Change the hearts and minds
    of those who deal in death,
    the drug pushers and salesmen
        who profit by the misery of others.
Free the people, Lord,
    from the slavery of drug addiction.

Loving Friend,
    so often we walk in darkness
        in the way we treat our brothers and sisters.
We can be blind to so much wrongdoing
    and acquiesce in so much injustice.
But you have taught us to walk another way;
    you have given us a new commandment
        which is the old command we had from your Father.
The way of love is the way of truth;
    the path of love is the path of light.
Let the darkness and its oppression pass away.
Lead us into the light
    that we may love our sisters and brothers
        and so doing reflect the beauty of your light.

RESPONSE
L: When kings and presidents defy your laws and oppress your people
R: may they learn to hear your voice and turn to new ways.

May the God who created the seas give you deep calm
May the God who created the stars give you radiant light
May the God who created people grant you many friendships
May the God who is your Father abide with you always

DAY 16

White riders of the dashing foam
Yellow waves of the swaying corn
Racing greys of the cloudy sky
Heralds of the great God of all creation

RESPONSORIAL PSALM: 119:41–42, 45–46

L: May your unfailing love come to me, O Lord,
    your salvation according to your promise;
R: then I will answer the one who taunts me,
    for I trust in your word.

L: I will walk about in freedom,
    for I have sought out your precepts.
R: I will speak of your statutes before kings
    and will not be put to shame.

AFFIRMATION AND PLEDGE: Section 6

READING: Exodus 4:1–9

MEDITATION

Signs – people seek them; many need them; some are terrified by them. We are told not to ask for signs but if God grants them it can be a great help and encouragement. But though there are signs to encourage there are also signs that fill people with apprehension. Those who walk in their own way, those who behave with pride, those who oppress the innocent, such people will find terror in the signs of God. Moses was faced with an obdurate oppressor. Such a one needed more than a word from the messenger of God. The signs which Moses did may appear a kind of magic but it soon became apparent that his was a power greater than magic, not his own power, but the mighty power of God.

'Then the Lord said, "If they do not believe you or pay attention to the first miraculous sign, they may believe the second." ' (4:8)

PRAYERS

Holy God,
    help us to understand your power
        and your way of turning the oppressor from his path.
    Help your church to find the right words
        to condemn the sin but recover the sinner.
    Let us not be afraid to utter your word of judgement
        and make us aware that we too stand under judgement.
    May we seek your mercy for those around us and for ourselves
        and be obedient to your divine will.

I recognise, Lord, that others need to be freed
    but I do not always recognise those things that enslave me.
Free me from anger that hurts
    all those around me.

Free me from anger that bursts into verbal violence
   against enemy, friend and relative.
Free me from anger that betrays you
   and denies the divine calling within me.
Free me from anger and help me to show
   the fruit of the Spirit,
      patience, kindness and self-control.

Risen Lord,
   bind us together in a family of love.
      May mothers and fathers know and teach truth;
      may young people overcome the evil around them;
      may children know the story of your love.
   Bind us together in a family of truth
      and a fellowship of holiness
         for the glory of your name.

RESPONSE

L: Lord God, your wisdom and love are seen in every generation;
R: help us to see and understand your signs in our time.

May God give you bread to satisfy your hunger
May God give you water to quench your thirst
May God who gave his Son to offer you salvation
Grant you his Spirit to enable you to serve him

DAY 17

Light reflected in the surface of the lake
Light reflected in the bottle's shining glass
Light reflected in the mirror's polished face
Christ's light reflected in a thousand tarnished lives

RESPONSORIAL PSALM: 119:49–50, 54–55

L: Remember your word to your servant,
     for you have given me hope.
R: My comfort in my suffering is this;
     your promise renews my life.

L: Your decrees are the theme of my song
     wherever I lodge.
R: In the night I remember your name, O Lord,
     and I will keep your law.

AFFIRMATION AND PLEDGE: Section 7

READING: Exodus 4:10–17

MEDITATION

It is a great encouragement to struggling disciples to find that Moses, the great national leader of the Israelites, did not consider himself a great speaker. But God enables whom he will, this one to speak, another one to act. Even when Moses is given the assurance he tries to evade the task. Send someone else. Isn't that so often our plea? There is a job to be done – but find someone else to do it.

Are there tasks that God is asking you to undertake? And are you responding to the call or evading his call? Moses was given an assurance that his brother would help but the greater assurance is that God will be with them both and will give them the words to speak. Trust God; he will not ask you to do something without giving you the guidance and gifts you need to accomplish the task.

' "Now go; I will help you speak and will teach you what to say." ' (4:12)

PRAYERS

Father,
     what are you asking us to do in a world of many needs?
     Sometimes a word of prophecy is needed;
          at other times a message of encouragement.
     How shall I say 'Thus speaks the Lord'
          unless I live close to you and trust you day by day?
     If I rely on my own wisdom, if I act in my own power,
          then I am weak and foolish.
     If I wait upon you in prayer
          then I can speak with a golden tongue
               and walk with the shepherd's staff.

Lord,
    release me from green-eyed envy
        that cannot rejoice in the good gifts of others
        but seeks to gain for myself
            all that is rightly theirs.
    Forgive me for looking with envy
        at all the beautiful possessions of my neighbour
        even though I have my own gifts and graces.
    Release me from the burden
        of longing for what is not my own
        when what is mine is delight enough
            both to enjoy and to share.

Merciful Redeemer,
    deliver us from all that degrades;
        from passion that abuses those we pretend to love;
        from seeing others as objects to be exploited;
        from pride that puts our own interests before our neighbour's;
        from a worldliness that lacks spiritual insight.
    Keep us firm in the faith
        and ready to do the will of your Father
            in whose presence we find our peace.

RESPONSE
    L: Father, there are many times when we feel weak and helpless;
    R: teach us what to say and how to act in your name.

May God give you light for your pilgrim way
May God give you music on your disciple's path
May God give you guidance through the maze of decision
May the Holy Trinity inspire you with courage and with hope

<table>
<tr><td>

DAY
18

</td><td>

Take away from me the yellow of cowardice and selfishness
Take away from me the scarlet of passion and pride
Give me the green of stewardship, care of the planet
Give me the blue of generosity, fruit of the Spirit

</td></tr>
</table>

RESPONSORIAL PSALM: 119:57–58, 63–64

L: You are my portion, O Lord;
　　I have promised to obey your words.
R: I have sought your face with all my heart;
*　　be gracious to me according to your promise.*

L: I am a friend to all who fear you,
　　to all who follow your precepts.
R: The earth is filled with your love, O Lord;
*　　teach me your decrees.*

READING: Exodus 5:1–14

MEDITATION

It is a strange fact of life that the oppressor does not see the writing on the wall but makes the oppression even harder. Eventually this leads to a complete change – a revolution. If Pharaoh had been willing to listen to the cries of the people or heeded the warnings of God, the people of Israel might well have stayed in Egypt. But he made the oppression worse and therefore made radical action inevitable. Now the people knew that they must leave with Moses and that the die was cast.

Many a situation of conflict and tension in our day could be resolved if the oppression were removed and a new and creative way of partnership sought, but too often repression is deep-rooted and open rebellion breaks out or the oppressed flee into a place of safety. Tyrants learn little from history.

' *"Make the work harder for the men so that they keep working".*' (5:9)

PRAYERS

Loving God,
　I bow before you in quiet prayer
　　for people who have suffered too much pain;
　　for those obliged to carry heavy burdens,
　　for those who have known the terror of oppression,
　　for those who have been through the fires of persecution,
　　for those who have been driven from their homes.
　Give them comfort in your presence
　　and may the day of liberty soon dawn for them.

　Help us, good Lord, to free our planet of pollution.
　　We have filled our homes and lungs with smoke,
　　we have fouled the rivers and seas with chemicals and waste,
　　we have filled the air with gases
　　　and allowed chimneys to belch out disease and death;

we have irradiated the planet
   and endangered our species;
we have obscured the truth about the dangers
   of such activities for ourselves and future generations.
Help us, good Lord, to repent
   and to free our planet of pollution.

Compassionate Shepherd,
   when we err from your way like lost sheep
      guide us back to safe ways and wholesome pastures.
   Help us to resist temptations and avoid snares.
   May we hold to the truth we have received
      and walk in the way of righteousness.
   May we affirm our faith in Father, Son and Spirit
      and enter into our inheritance, eternal life,
         when you come again in glory
            to welcome us into your kingdom.

THE LORD'S PRAYER

RESPONSE
   L: When tyrants oppress and lay heavy burdens on your people
   R: Lord, lead us into the quiet revolution and the era of peace.

   The peace of the deep sea calm be yours
   The peace of the deep forest quiet be yours
   The peace of the mystic's inner silence be yours
   The peace of the blessed Three be yours
      To eternity

DAY 19

Oak leaves, pine needles, red berries, rose hips,
Daisies and dandelions, carpet of grass,
Stones in the brook, waterfalls, wide flowing rivers
All speak of God, Creator and Friend

RESPONSORIAL PSALM: 119:65–66, 71–72

L: Do good to your servant according to your word, O Lord.
R: Teach me knowledge and good judgement, for I believe in your commands.

L: It was good for me to be afflicted
    so that I might learn your decrees.
R: The law from your mouth is more precious to me
    than thousands of pieces of silver and gold.

READING: Exodus 6:1–9

MEDITATION

Pharaoh, the power of the state, is of no account before the power of God.
When God speaks, Pharaoh must let the people go. He may have a purpose in
his own mind to keep them as slaves but his word, his will, his mighty army
cannot withstand the word of God.

In many generations we see the conflict between the power of the state and the
power of God – not simply the church; the church when true to its calling is simply
an instrument of God's purpose. In Russia, in South Africa, in South and Central
America, economic and political power seek to defy the will of God. Always in
the end the purpose of God will be worked out; oppressive systems fall and new
eras begin. So in our day may God speak: 'Let my people go.'

' *"I am the Lord, and I will bring you out from under the yoke of the Egyptians".*' (6:6)

PRAYERS

Holy Lord,
    it is not always easy for us to trust your promises.
    We know that you are faithful to your people;
        what you promise you will perform.
    Yet we are so often faithless, doubting.
    We long for liberation; we pray for liberation,
        but we do not hear your word promising freedom
            or we do not trust it.
    Forgive us for the failures of the past
        and make us ready to trust you more in the future.

    May we be freed, Lord God, from waterborne diseases.
    Water should be pure and life-giving;
        in so many places it is impure
        and a carrier of death.
    Rivers and lakes should be healthy for fish and people;
        they have become a breeding ground for disease
            and a destroyer of the life chain for other species.

Pure water should be abundantly available
    to quench the thirst of your people.
For many it has become a rare commodity,
    so many people die.
May the rivers be made pure,
    the lakes and seas respected.
May we become good stewards
    of the precious gift of water
that your people may have life
    and have it more abundantly.

Crucified Saviour,
    we put our trust in you
        for you make us pure as you are pure.
    Deliver us from lawlessness and unrighteousness;
        lead us in the way of obedience and truth.
    We do not know what we shall be
        but we pray that when you return in glory
    you will make us like yourself
        and receive us into your kingdom.

RESPONSE
L: Holy God, when we experience situations of despair
R: give us new hope and vision through your word.

May the Father who made you guide you in his way
May the Son who loves you inspire you each day
May the Spirit who fills you answer your deepest prayer
May the Holy Trinity surround you with his care

DAY 20

Light of the dawn, rose-coloured glory
Light of noonday, bright in the heavens
Light of the evening, soft amongst shadows
Light of the night, star bright in the dark
Reflecting the light of God, Creator and King

RESPONSORIAL PSALM: 119:73–74, 76–77

L: Your hands made me and formed me;
         give me understanding to learn your commands.
R: May they who fear you rejoice when they see me,
         for I have put my hope in your word.

L: May your unfailing love be my comfort,
         according to your promise to your servant.
R: Let your compassion come to me that I may live,
         for your law is my delight.

READING: Exodus 7:1–13

MEDITATION

   The ways of God are beyond our human understanding; in history and human affairs the divine pattern is woven. It seems at times that one chapter denies another in the story of Exodus; yet the story being completed shows that this is not so. God sends Moses with the message to let his people go; but he also hardens the heart of Pharaoh so that he will not respond – not yet. The response will come when God is ready for it, when he has prepared Pharaoh and the Israelites for his great purpose.
   So it is in today's world. The pattern is not always clear. There are sufferings and setbacks. The hearts of many are hardened but when God is ready all will work out according to his divine plan. Trust God – and never cease to wonder that he trusts you to do his work.

' *"Though I multiply my miraculous signs and wonders in Egypt, he will not listen to you."* '
(7:3)

PRAYERS

   Righteous Father,
      our world is full of tyranny;
         there are hard taskmasters who refuse to obey you.
      In many lands your people are oppressed and persecuted.
   Lord,
      hear the cry of the needy and the poor.
      Change the minds and hearts of tyrants
         that they may give freedom and justice in the land.
      When tyrants remain obdurate, act with your divine power
         to bring liberation for your people.
   Lord,
      may we see your signs and wonders in our generation.

Help us, good Lord, to be free
    of the terrors of disease.
Give us a healthy regard for our bodies
    and all our physical and mental needs.
Grant skill and patience to doctors and nurses
    that they may help the process of recovery.
Give us a quiet confidence in your healing grace
    as we wait on you in quiet meditation.
So grant us health of body, mind and spirit
    for the glory of your name.

Merciful Redeemer,
    help us to respond to your love
        which is so deep and wonderful
            and makes us children of God our Father.
Inspire us to express that love to others.
You held nothing back
    but gave your life for our sakes.
May we be ready to sacrifice
    in order to give to brothers and sisters in need.
May our love be expressed not only in words and intentions
    but in sincere works of compassion.
What we have received and heard from the beginning
    may we express in proclaiming the good news of love
        in speech and action to the glory of God our Father.

RESPONSE
    L: When oppressors refuse to turn from their evil ways
    R: they bring sorrow to the people and judgement on themselves.

May the Father walk with you in the quiet of the garden
May the Son accompany you on the Emmaus road
May the Spirit be your guide on the road to Gaza
May the blessed Trinity, Father, Son and Spirit,
   be with you on your pilgrim way

DAY 21

Pebbles on the beach, smoothed round by the sea
Stones on the road, sharp-edged to the foot
Rocks on the mountain, majestic in splendour
Shapes of creation, made for God's glory

RESPONSORIAL PSALM: 119:81–82, 88

    L: My soul faints with longing for your salvation,
        but I have put my hope in your word.
    R: My eyes fail, looking for your promise;
        I say, 'When will you comfort me?'

    L: Preserve my life according to your love,
    R: and I will obey the statutes of your mouth.

READING: Exodus 7:14–25

MEDITATION

    When the oppressor will not move from his oppression, then the plagues become worse. God deals dramatically with the Egyptians, turning the water to blood as a warning. But Pharaoh does not want to listen and the people dig for water elsewhere. People can avoid the plainest signs from God and refuse to obey him. They thus bring on themselves worse things.

    In situations of oppression today there are many ways in which people both within and outside the situation seek to act for justice. Symbolically, peacefully, the appeal is made to the oppressor. Yet the call is disregarded. This can lead to much worse persuasion when people rise up in violent revolution to overcome oppression. How much better it would be if the peaceful signs were heeded.

' "With the staff that is in my hand I will strike the water of the Nile, and it will be changed into blood." ' (7:17)

PRAYERS

    Lord,
        how sad it is when people come to their senses
            only by acts of power and judgement.
        How sad it is that they will not hear your word
            nor respond to your mercy with mercy.
        How sad it is that people are determined
            to carry on in a way of self-destruction.
    Lord,
        may people be more ready to respond to the signs of the rainbow
            that they may not experience the sign of blood.

    Some tell me, Lord, that work makes free;
        at times in history that has been an ironic lie
            for slave work has led to disease and death.
    But there is dignity in worthwhile labour,
        in work carried out well, not just for wages
            but for the common good.

It is an indignity when no work is available,
   when a parent cannot properly feed or house children
      because there is no employment.
Lord,
   free us from the scourge of unemployment;
      may there be worthwhile and rewarding work
         for all who are ready to undertake it.
   So may our life together be enabled
      by work well done for the welfare of all
         and for the glory of your name.

Loving Friend,
   You are the way and the truth;
      we pray that you will keep us in your way
         and help us to receive and understand the truth.
   We have received great gifts from the Father
      when we have sought to do what pleases him.
   It is his delight that we should put our trust in you
      and that we should love each other.
   Doing so, we are made one with you
      and the Spirit, the Father's gift, dwells in us.
   May we find our peace
      in communion with the Father, the Son and the Spirit.

RESPONSE

   L: Lord, when tyrants refuse to turn from wickedness
   R: you grieve to see them walk in the way of destruction.

   As the grains of sand on the shore are innumerable
   As the stars in the sky are myriad
   As the drops in the ocean are countless
   So may God bless you abundantly, day by day

Lord, I take off the mask I wear before strangers
Lord, I put away the mask I wear among friends
Lord, I take off the mask I wear even with my family
So, revealing my true face, I stand before you,
my Saviour and my faithful friend

RESPONSORIAL PSALM: 119:89–94

L: Your word, O Lord, is eternal;
     it stands firm in the heavens.
R: Your faithfulness continues through all generations;
     you established the earth, and it endures.

L: Your laws endure to this day,
     for all things serve you.
R: If your law had not been my delight,
     I would have perished in my affliction.

L: I will never forget your precepts,
     for by them you have renewed my life.
R: Save me, for I am yours;
     I have sought out your precepts.

READING: Exodus 11:1–10

MEDITATION

When people refuse to see the signs how terrible is the result. Here we find that the many plagues to warn Pharaoh have their culmination in the death of the first-born sons of all the Egyptians. There is widespread grief and lamentation but this time it is amongst the Egyptians not amongst the Israelites who had suffered at their hands for so long. What are we to make of this? The Passover is a great celebration feast for the Israelites for this is the day of their deliverance, but it is a great day of mourning for the Egyptians for this marks the time of their suffering.

Is this then the way that God deals with obdurate people? Is he a God of wrath and judgement rather than a God of mercy and forgiveness? Or is it true to say that he is both, for he is ready to forgive and be merciful but if people reject his offer of forgiveness and continue in the way of evil, they bring destruction on themselves? Read and meditate on this great action of history and learn from this – that there was greater lamentation in Egypt than they had ever known before, because they persisted in oppression in defiance of the living God.

' *"There will be loud wailing throughout Egypt – worse than there has ever been or ever will be again."* ' (11:6)

PRAYERS

Lord,
    we keep a space of silence
        for all those who suffer a deep grief.
    Though tyrants may bring disaster on themselves,

though oppressors may deserve their own destruction,
yet when there is mourning in the land
    we feel for those who are in sorrow,
    we grieve with those who grieve
    and we pray that their experience
        may bring a change of heart and mind.
Lord, in your mercy hear our prayer.

Loving God,
    there are many people who are exiled,
      far from home and friends,
        driven out by harsh regimes and cruel tyrants.
    Forgive us that we acquiesce too easily
      in the growing number of refugees,
      and that so often we offer no welcome.
    May there come a time
      when every family, every person is able
      to live happily and freely in the country
        which is their home
      and, until that time, may there always be
        cities of refuge, places of sanctuary,
      where a home and welcome
        is offered in your name.

Righteous Mediator,
    guard and protect us from false spirits,
      from the spirit of error, the spirit of negativity,
      the spirit of pride and the spirit of envy.
    Help us to test the spirits
      to know whether they are from you.
    We believe that you were sent by your Father
      to become flesh and dwell among us.
    The spirit of error seeks to move us from this truth
      and the worldly minded seek to destroy our faith.
    Guide us that we may discern
        the spirit of truth and the spirit of error
      and affirm the one and reject the other,
        that we may be known as the children of God.

RESPONSE
L: Holy God, when evil people close their ears and hearts to you
R: they bring sorrow to the world and to themselves.

May the Great One who is both mother and father bless you
May the Suffering Servant who is both brother and sister bless you
May the Great Spirit who is neither male nor female bless you
The blessing of the Trinity, the Great Mystery,
  be yours now and always

Lines across the field, furrows of beauty
Lines across the sea, waves of never-ending splendour
Lines across the sky, clouds of the stratosphere
Lines from people to people, connections of love

RESPONSORIAL PSALM: 119:97–98, 101–104

L: Oh, how I love your law!
     I meditate on it all day long.
R: Your commands make me wiser than my enemies,
     for they are ever with me.

L: I have kept my feet from every evil path
     so that I might obey your word.
R: I have not departed from your laws,
     for you yourself have taught me.

L: How sweet are your promises to my taste,
     sweeter than honey to my mouth!
R: I gain understanding from your precepts;
     therefore I hate every wrong path.

READING: Exodus 12:1–13

MEDITATION

     This is the feast of the Lord's Passover, commemoration of God's preservation
of the people of Israel and this is the continued feast of the people in every
generation since. It points to the great devotion of the Jewish people. It also raises
afresh the great questions of life. During the time of the holocaust the Jewish
people continued to keep the Passover yet the people suffered terribly, becoming
themselves the sacrificial lamb as they were driven to their deaths in millions.
     Who can probe such deep mysteries and know the answers to the deep
questions? Yet the Jew knows in his heart that God delivered his people from
slavery at the time of the Passover and the Christian knows that God so loved his
world that Jesus was sent to be the Passover lamb for all people, that by the blood of
his sacrifice people might be freed from the slavery of sin.

' *"Eat it in haste; it is the Lord's Passover."* ' (12:11)

PRAYERS
     Lord,
          the commemorations are precious to us;
               the remembering of deliverance for your people, Israel,
                    in the great Exodus from Egypt;
               the remembering of those who perished
                    in the holocaust in Europe;
               the remembering of the suffering of your Son
                    on the cross of Calvary;
               the remembering each time we share together in the thanksgiving,
                    in the feast of Holy Communion.

Help us to remember not only for the past
but to consecrate the future to you.

Good Shepherd,
how sad it is
when some of your people are enslaved by oppressive regimes,
and exploited on the grounds of race.
We confess that we too easily
have given way to racist thoughts and actions.
Lead us to the place of freedom
where every person is accepted as an individual
whatever their race, colour or country
and where we recognise that we are all one family,
looking to one Father,
our Redeemer, Friend and Lord.

Dearest Brother,
you came amongst us
to show us the way of love.
You are the expression of the Father's love.
Help us to love each other
for love comes from God.
The summit of love is not our love for God
but the Father's love for us
in sending you to take away our sins
by your perfect sacrifice.
We cannot see the glory of our Creator
but we can have communion with him
when we love one another.
So grant us the bliss of union
with the Father, with you, the Son and with the Holy Spirit,
one God now and for ever.

RESPONSE

L: Lord, when you call your people to the journey of liberation
R: make them ready to respond with speed and gladness.

May God who made the rivers, seas and oceans bless you
May God who made the fields, the hills and mountains bless you
May God who made all creatures, wild and tame, bless you
May God, Father, Son and Spirit bless you now and always

DAY 24

I hear the noise of the waterfall, the sound of many waters
I hear the beating of wings, the sound of many birds
I hear the voice of God, words clearly spoken
*   and my whole being becomes quiet, listening to God's word*

RESPONSORIAL PSALM: 119:105–108, 111–112

L: Your word is a lamp to my feet
    and a light for my path.
R: I have taken an oath and confirmed it,
    that I will follow your righteous laws.

L: I have suffered much;
    renew my life, O Lord, according to your word.
R: Accept, O Lord, the willing praise of my mouth,
    and teach me your laws.

L: Your statutes are my heritage for ever; they are the joy of my heart.
R: My heart is set on keeping your decrees to the very end.

READING: Exodus 12:14–28

MEDITATION

It is important to keep the feast; it is important to recall deliverance. The Jew remembers on the day of Passover all that God did for his people; the Christian remembers at the Lord's Supper all that God has done for us in Christ. It is easier to remember in days of suffering; it is harder to remember in days of prosperity, yet one should continue to remember in all the varied circumstances of life and in every generation the saving acts of our God. That nation will not prosper which is unmindful of God. Those people will not find true happiness who forget God's presence and his gifts. Think often of all that God has accomplished for you.

' *"This is a day you are to commemorate; for the generations to come you shall celebrate it as a festival to the Lord."* ' (12:14)

PRAYERS

So often, Lord, our remembering is of times of sorrow—
    we recall the suffering of those who died in war;
    we remember the oppression of past generations;
    we recall the torture of the martyrs, your persecuted people;
    we remember the suffering of our Lord on Calvary.
Help us to remember too the times of rejoicing,
    the deliverance of your people from Egypt,
    the ending of war and the reign of peace,
    the liberation that has come to so many in our own generation,
    the joy of the resurrection day for your disciples.
Help us to be the Easter people,
    rejoicing in all that you do for us in Christ.

Holy God,
   you created your people in your own image, male and female.
   You created us to love one another
      and to share in the joy of your creation.
   It is a betrayal when we ill treat each other
      or when we practise domination of one sex by another.
   Forgive us for the harsh treatment of women
      in so many places, through so many generations.
   May we give to women a proper place in our society,
      recognising their talents and gifts equally alongside men
         and accepting our common task
            to work for the mutual good in our society.

Risen Lord,
   you have filled our lives with joy
      by your precious gift of the Holy Spirit.
   Filled with the Spirit
      we can proclaim our faith
         that you are the Saviour of the world.
   We are made one with you through love
      and abiding in that love
         we dwell with God our Father.
   Love makes perfect for the final reckoning.
   When we have love we are not afraid
      for perfect love overcomes all fear.
   We love you and, responsive to your teaching,
      we seek to love our neighbours.
   Your Father desires that we show our love for him
      by the depth of our love for one another.
   So may our love be a sign of your presence.

RESPONSE

   L: Loving Shepherd, let us never forget your great mercy
   R: in leading your people out of slavery to the Promised Land.

   Let the streets of the city be filled with joy
   Let the houses of the city echo with praise
   Let the people of the city show love to one another
   May the city be a place of peace and that peace be yours always

DAY 25

Eyes open to the beauty of the world of nature
Ears open to the myriad sounds of creation
Lips open to praise the God who made us
Hearts open to receive him into our lives

RESPONSORIAL PSALM: 119:113–114, 116–117

L: I hate double-minded men, but I love your law.
R: You are my refuge and my shield;
I have put my hope in your word.

L: Sustain me according to your promise, and I shall live;
do not let my hopes be dashed.
R: Uphold me, and I shall be delivered;
I shall always have regard for your decrees.

READING: Exodus 12:29–42

MEDITATION

The deliverance is in the Exodus when all the people left the land of Egypt.
Yet this is no simple matter if the historical account is to be believed. The Israelites
had been in Egypt for 430 years, many generations. Around one million people
left as refugees to journey into the unknown. This was a massive exodus.

In modern times this is like the exodus of the Kurds from Iraq, fleeing before
the violent tyranny of Saddam Hussein; hundreds of thousands of Kurds
headed for Turkey and Iran and most stayed on the frontier mountains where
many died, as they waited for safe havens to be found for them.

The logistics of such great migrations of people are complex. It is easier if
oppression can be ended, allowing people to stay rather than being driven out
to unfamiliar places. But for Israel the divine plan was to bring them to the
Promised Land. So began one of the greatest migrations of history – the exodus
of the Jews from Egypt.

'All the Lord's divisions left Egypt.' (12:41)

PRAYERS

God of Moses and Miriam,
we are filled with joy when we recall
all those who have gone from slavery to freedom.
We remember the great exodus of your people from Egypt,
we see the gathering in to Israel of the many people
who have suffered in Eastern Europe;
we see those who have moved from places of oppression
in the Americas, in Asia, in Africa,
to places of sanctuary.
Lord, we give you thanks that the day of liberation
has dawned for so many people;
we pray that soon all tyranny and persecution may be ended
and your people live in freedom and harmony throughout the world.

O Lord,
   how we need to be free from the demands of an ideology
      which disregards the needs of ordinary people,
      which exalts prestige at the expense of dignity,
      which prefers pride to helping the poor,
      which exacts a toll from working people
         to give glory to the political ideas of an élite.
   Lord, we hold before you all those
      who have suffered oppression and persecution
         because of the ideology of political demagogues.
   Restore a true perspective to the leaders of all nations
      that we may seek the ways of justice and of peace.

Loving Lord Jesus,
   we know that you are the promised Messiah, Christ the King;
   placing our trust in you we become children of God
      and since we love our Father we love all of his children.
   In love we take our delight in obeying God's will
      and our obedience is both cause and fruit of love.
   We believe that you are the Christ, the Son of God,
      and that faith gives us victory in the world,
         a victory over greed, hatred and enmity.
   Since we are born of God we are born to love,
      and in reaching the summit of love
         we experience communion with God.

THE LORD'S PRAYER

RESPONSE

   L: Lord, when the day of liberation dawns
   R: no tyrant can prevent the spreading of the light.

   Be still and wait on God
   May the silence of the Creator enfold you
   May the silence of the Redeemer surround you
   May the silence of the Comforter encircle you
   May the silence of the blessed Three
      surround you to eternity

DAY 26

The Father with you in the way of creating
The Son with you in the way of loving
The Spirit with you in the way of giving
The Trinity alongside you in the way of living

RESPONSORIAL PSALM: 119:121–124, 127–128

L: I have done what is righteous and just;
   do not leave me to my oppressors.
R: Ensure your servant's well-being;
   let not the arrogant oppress me.

L: My eyes fail, looking for your salvation,
   looking for your righteous promise.
R: Deal with your servant according to your love
   and teach me your decrees.

L: Because I love your commands
   more than gold, more than pure gold,
R: and because I consider all your precepts right,
   I hate every wrong path.

READING: Exodus 13:17–22

MEDITATION

God gives guiding signs to his people. The Exodus was a great national event of enormous importance in the history and survival of the people. So the guiding signs are dramatic, sensational. A great pillar of cloud guided the people by day. Natural phenomena can be strange and remarkable. The dust pillars formed in certain areas; cloud formations that are most unusual in shape. Such a pillar is conceivable. But what of the pillar of fire by night, this guiding light in the darkness? It is not easy to think of any natural phenomenon to explain such a happening. But then we find in religious experience that divine intervention is natural and God finds ways of freeing his people and guiding his people. Such great signs are necessary and comprehensible for such great national events – but God gives his guiding signs for you too. Be ready for the signs.

'By day the Lord went ahead of them in a pillar of cloud to guide them on their way and by night in a pillar of fire.' (13:21)

PRAYERS

How much we need your guidance, holy God,
   when we wander in the wilderness of our modern world,
   in the midst of secularism, in the places of oppression,
   before the practice of the occult,
      when there is so much evil in our world.
Go before us as a pillar of cloud
   to lead us in the way of righteousness.
Go before us as a pillar of fire
   to renew your people in dedication and trust.

Show us the way we should go
     and help us to walk in it for your name's sake.

Righteous Father,
   we confess before you
      that suffering has been brought into the lives of your people
         by religious bigotry
   and pray your forgiveness
      for intolerance and lack of understanding.
   We hold before you too
      all those who have been the victims of strange cults
      and the terrible blasphemy of the occult.
   May your Holy Spirit cast out all that is evil
      and overcome the forces of darkness.
   May we seek what is true, righteous and pure
      and find in your presence
         the peace that passes understanding.

Blessed Redeemer,
   you came by water and blood into the world
      and by water and blood you gave up your life.
   The Spirit brooding over creation
      watched over your birth and your death.
   The Spirit, the water and the blood,
      all are witnesses to the truth
         that you are the Christ, the Son of God,
            by whose death comes our life.

RESPONSE

   L: Holy God, however difficult the way in the journey of liberation
   R: you will guide your people by signs and wonders.

   May the pillar of fire that led the Israelites be your guide
   May the star that shone over Bethlehem be your guide
   May the voice that spoke to Samuel be your guide
   May the voice that challenged Paul be your guide
   May the living God be your companion through all your days

DAY 27

Bright Lord of the dawn, be with us in our worship
May the light of your Son shine on us
May the life of your Spirit be in us
Holy Trinity, enable and enthuse us, inspire and use us

RESPONSORIAL PSALM: 119:129–130, 133–146

L: Your statutes are wonderful;
    therefore I obey them.
R: The entrance of your words gives light;
    it gives understanding to the simple.

L: Direct my footsteps according to your word;
    let no sin rule over me.
R: Redeem me from the oppression of men,
    that I may obey your precepts.

L: Make your face shine upon your servant
    and teach me your decrees.
R: Streams of tears flow from my eyes,
    for your law is not obeyed.

READING: Exodus 14:5–31

MEDITATION

    The mighty hand of God is seen for the deliverance of the people of Israel and the destruction of the Egyptians. Is this myth or history, fact or fantasy? There is no doubt that for the Israelites it is an historical part of the great story of liberation, treasured and commemorated through centuries. Viewed from another perspective, this event has been recorded by gypsies as a tragic destruction of their people. Some scholars have tried to explain the account by natural phenomena that occur in the region. Others regard it as highly coloured history, a mythical account of deliverance. But that something happened to turn seemingly inevitable defeat into actual deliverance seems undoubted. That God delivered his people is clear to the Jews. Meditate on this and be assured that God acts for his people.

'All that night the Lord drove the sea back with a strong east wind and turned it into dry land. The waters were divided.' (14:21)

PRAYERS

    Lord God,
        the earth is yours for you made it,
            the sea and the dry land are your creation.
        To you belongs the glory of the planets
            and the changing of the seasons.
        You control the winds and you give the rain.
        What appears to us as a great miracle
            is the working out of your mighty purpose.

Since you called the earth into being
and made the seas and the dry land to have their place
so you can make the sea to be dry land
and cover the dry land with seas.
Nothing is beyond your purpose of wisdom and love.
To you be the glory, Lord of heaven and earth.

Prince of Peace,
deliver us from the scourge of war.
In generation after generation
for causes good and bad
your people have engaged in conflict
and there has been a terrible cost in suffering and death.
Forgive us for resorting to war.
Help us to overcome injustice
by action which is not violent;
help us to pursue the path of peace,
resolving differences by conciliation.
Lord Jesus, free us from the violence of war;
and lead us in your path of peace.

Righteous Mediator,
You are the bridge between us and God;
we have received this faith from people
but the greater testimony comes to us from God.
Your Father bears witness to you,
and this is the good news we receive—
that God has given us eternal life
and this abundant life is found in you, Lord Jesus.
If we turn from you we lose life;
if we turn to you we gain life.
Praise be to God for his most wonderful gifts.

RESPONSE
L: Lord, when the way to freedom seems impossible
R: help us to trust you for the miracle of grace.

May the insects in the soil speak to you of God
May the fish in the sea speak to you of God
May the birds of the air speak to you of God
May the cattle in the fields speak to you of God
May you know the presence of God around you by day and by night

DAY 28

Lord of the rivers, flow through our lives with righteousness
God of the seas, refresh our hearts with holiness
Lord of the oceans, renew us with the depths of your compassion
Living water of life, refresh our inner being

RESPONSORIAL PSALM: 119:137–138, 141–144

L: Righteous are you, O Lord,
    and your laws are right.
R: The statutes you have laid down are righteous;
    they are fully trustworthy.

L: Though I am lowly and despised,
    I do not forget your precepts.
R: Your righteousness is everlasting
    and your law is true.

L: Trouble and distress have come upon me,
    but your commands are my delight.
R: Your statutes are for ever right;
    give me understanding that I may live.

READING: Exodus 16:1–36

MEDITATION

The way of liberation is not always an easy way. Sometimes it may seem that the situation of slavery is easier to bear than the path of freedom. There is a certain security in the provision given by the oppressor; there is a risk in the way of the unknown. So Israel grumbles. At least in Egypt they had bread; now they starve in the wilderness.

But God who brings about the liberty provides manna in the wilderness. He does not let his people starve. The provision is sufficient for the day. They are not to store up for the future. Only on the day before the Sabbath was enough provided for two days.

We must learn to trust God. Whatever enslaves you, let go and let God bring you liberation. Be assured that God will provide for your needs; travel in trust; travel simply; journey freely; know that God goes with you.

'The Israelites ate manna for forty years, until they came to a land that was settled.' (16:35)

PRAYERS

Holy Father,
    you provide for the needs of all your people.
    In the productivity of planet earth
        there is sufficient for every person to eat and be satisfied.
    We confess that we in our foolishness
        have caused hunger, disease and distress.
    We have not been careful to cultivate the earth
        nor caring in sharing its products.

58

You have given us a fruitful creation
and the means to cross the continents
making this one world, our planet earth.
Teach us the way of sharing;
give us a sense of the right priorities
that the hungry of all nations may be fed
and your name honoured in all places of our world.

Creator God,
you are the giver of all good
and we are simply stewards of all that we possess.
Yet too often evil people make the might of money
a cause of oppression of the needy and the poor.
Economic power is wielded like a weapon
and hurt inflicted on vulnerable communities.
We hold before you all those
whose lives have been threatened
and whose homes have been wrecked
and whose communities have been divided
by those controlling the economy.
Forgive this misuse of power
and lead us all in the way of caring,
the path of sharing,
that the common good may be advanced
and your name honoured in our time.

Crucified Saviour,
You have given us confidence
to come before the throne of grace with our requests.
Help us to pray wisely according to your will
for then we know our requests are answered.
We pray for brothers and sisters in trouble and need
that you may guide, heal and bless them.
We pray for brothers and sisters who have done wrong
that they may repent and receive your forgiveness.
May we all turn from the errors of our path;
forgiven and free, may we walk in your way
for we ask it in your precious name.

RESPONSE

L: Loving Shepherd, there are times when for some it seems there will be no
food;
R: *since you provide for the needs of all your people,*
help us to share your gifts.

May the Father, Creator of the Universe, bless you in the morning of life
May the Son, Prince of Peace, bless you in the noon of discipleship
May the Spirit, Enabler and Comforter, bless you in the evening of your days
May the blessed Trinity be with you at the rising of the sun and at its going down

<table>
<tr><td>

DAY 29

</td><td>

White sands of the seashore endlessly stretching
Blue ridges of the high mountains far in the distance
Golden corn of the fields on the wide plain
Myriad stars of the Milky Way in the vault of the night sky
Speak of the glory of God, the vital life force

</td></tr>
</table>

RESPONSORIAL PSALM: 119:145–148, 153–154

L: I call with all my heart; answer me, O Lord,
       and I will obey your decrees.
R: I call out to you; save me and I will keep your statutes.

L: I rise before dawn and cry for help;
       I have put my hope in your word.
R: My eyes stay open through the watches of the night,
       that I may meditate on your promises.

L: Look upon my suffering and deliver me,
       for I have not forgotten your law.
R: Defend my cause and redeem me;
       renew my life according to your promise.

READING: Exodus 17:1–7

MEDITATION

As the Lord provided food, so the Lord provided water. Forty years in the wilderness he provided for his people. This was no life of luxury; it was a hard travelling life but the basics for survival were given, food and water.

So often we do not trust God. We are not ready to be liberated. We are not prepared for days of tough travelling. When we venture forward in faith, like Peter we suddenly hesitate in disbelief. We wonder whether God truly will protect, truly will provide. The Israelites found it was so, but they had to wander forty years in the wilderness before they came to the Promised Land. We expect the Promised Land without waiting, without wandering, without cost. Meditate on the years of the wilderness and learn to trust God whatever risks or uncertainties come your way.

' *"Strike the rock, and water will come out of it."* ' (17:6)

PRAYERS

How sad it is when children die for lack of pure water;
       how sad that so many suffer from diseases
             caused by water that is polluted.
Dear Lord, you have given us streams and rivers;
       you send the refreshing rain from heaven.
There should be water enough for all people.
We spend our money with motives of pride or power
       rather than providing water for villages and towns.
We waste the earth with our destructive technology
       rather than applying our skills to life-saving inventions.

Lord, forgive us and help us to become partners with you
    in preserving and using all that is good in your creation.
May there be pure water for all the people of your world
    that everyone may live healthily to the glory of your name.

Lord,
    forgive the dishonesty which puts ordinary people at risk
        to maintain vested interests
            or to protect the reputation of the powerful.
    Forgive those who for the sake of profit
        put at risk whole communities by radiation
        and adversely affect the health of children
            through the infecting of water
            or the pollution of the air.
    Help us to be more honest in our dealings with each other
        and more ready to accept the cost of mistakes
    that the health of the community may be preserved and protected.

Dearest Brother,
        protect us from evil influences which attack our faith;
        deliver us from evil powers which seek to overcome us;
        liberate our world from the evil which besets it.
    Since we come to new birth through you
        help us to behave as children of light
        and to know that our lives are safely held
            in the hands of God, our Father and our Friend.

RESPONSE

L: Lord of creation, you give us pure water to drink;
R: may we always be thankful for the gifts we receive from you.

The blessing of the One be with you in your solitude
The blessing of the Three be with you in community
The blessing of the Creator refresh you in your discipleship
The blessing of Father, Son and Spirit
    keep you in the communion of saints

DAY 30

The Lord God created the rock, granite face of the mountain
The Lord God created the iron, mineral product of the earth
The Lord God created the pearl, hidden gem of the ocean
Creator God, be present in your beauty and your power

RESPONSORIAL PSALM: 119:161–162, 165–166, 169–170, 175–176

L: Rulers persecute me without cause,
   but my heart trembles at your word.
R: I rejoice in your promise
   like one who finds great spoil.

L: Great peace have they who love your law,
   and nothing can make them stumble.
R: I wait for your salvation, O Lord,
   and I follow your commands.

L: May my cry come before you, O Lord;
   give me understanding according to your word.
R: May my supplication come before you;
   deliver me according to your promise.

L: Let me live that I may praise you,
   and may your laws sustain me.
R: I have strayed like a lost sheep.
   Seek your servant, for I have not forgotten your commandments.

READING: Exodus 20:1–20

MEDITATION

God delivers his people; God brings about their liberation but not to give them a life of licence, not that they may live any way they please. God is holy and calls his people to live holy lives. Enshrined in the ten commandments we have set down the way to worship God purely, the way to give honour within our family and the way to treat each other within the community. God's people are called to live peaceable and pure lives, at one with their neighbours, and at one with God.

God delivers his people today, from political oppression, from economic oppression, from racism, not that we may then turn the tables and oppress others but that we might be free to worship God and to care for one another. May there be a dawn of liberation for all the peoples of our world and may we live together in justice and in peace.

' "*I am the Lord your God, who brought you out of Egypt, out of the land of slavery.*" ' (20:2)

PRAYERS

Holy Lord God,
   you lead us in the way of righteousness
      and you teach us your truth.

You bring us from slavery
   into the land of promise.
Help us to turn from all that has enslaved us
   and to put our trust in you for freedom and for peace.
May we find our joy in walking in your way
   and in the beauty of holiness.
Help us to live in the way that you have taught us
   and to fulfil your loving purpose for us.
May we so serve you in this life
   that we may find our promised land in your eternal kingdom.

Lord God,
   deliver your people from tyranny in all its forms.
May we be free from political tyranny
   which despises the ordinary people;
may we be free from economic oppression
   which disregards the needs of the poor;
may we be free from religious persecution
   which denies our right to worship you.
May there come for all your people
   the day of liberation,
   the new dawn of freedom,
   the blessing of peace with justice
that your name may be hallowed
   wherever your people live.

Loving Lord Jesus,
   help us to turn from the idols of our generation,
      the idols of steel, of silver and of gold,
      the idols of materialism, of greed, of wealth.
Inspire us to understand the truth
   and by the truth may we be set free.
You came into our world
   to show us the way, the truth, the life;
may we find the way, know the truth
   and experience the life that is eternal
      through the love of God, Father, Son and Holy Spirit
         to whom be glory, now and always.

RESPONSE
   L: Father, there may be many times of slavery and oppression;
   R: may we trust you to lead us into freedom and peace.

May you be blessed by the God of Moses
   who witnessed with awe the burning bush
May you be blessed by the God of Moses
   who spoke with courage God's word to Pharaoh
May you be blessed by the God of Moses
   who led his people to the Promised Land

PRAYERS
OF PILGRIMAGE

Readings from the Acts of the Apostles. This is a lively account of the early church responding to the commission of Jesus with the guidance and power of the Holy Spirit. It is an account of the practical details and difficulties of the church but also of the signs and wonders that accompanied faithful proclamation. There is much to be learned about individual discipleship and the mission of the church in contemporary society through this dramatic account.
Some of the other prayers are based on the Song of Solomon and Philippians.

DAY 31

Lord God, where shall I be and find you not?
You are in the heavens and on the earth
You are in the heights and in the depths
In all places, in all situations,
I find that you are with me

RESPONSORIAL PSALM: 84:1–4

L: How lovely is your dwelling-place, O Lord Almighty!
    My soul yearns, even faints for the courts of the Lord;
R: my heart and my flesh cry out for the living God.

L: Even the sparrow has found a home,
    and the swallow a nest for herself, where she may have her young –
R: a place near your altar,
    O Lord Almighty, my King and my God.

L: Blessed are those who dwell in your house;
R: they are ever praising you.

READING: Acts 1:1–11

MEDITATION

Jesus calls us to be witnesses for him, but so often we miss the mark. We fail to speak of what we consider most important in life. Why do we hesitate? Is it because we lack confidence or wisdom or power? Yet the promise is power! The world finds power in money, in bombs and in alliances but that is not the promised power from Jesus. He gives us spiritual power; he promises us the gift of the Spirit. Should we not welcome our baptism in the Spirit? Do we doubt the promise of Jesus or fear its consequences? We cannot be witnesses for Christ unless we receive the guidance and gifts of the Spirit. Once we have entered into the promises we shall join the company of those who have gone out in ever-widening circles with the invocation, Come, Holy Spirit, come!

' *"You will receive power when the Holy Spirit comes on you; and you will be my witnesses".'*
(1: 8)

PRAYERS

Creator God,
    you sent your Son to redeem the world.
He gave himself completely, holding nothing back.
    In his dying is our rising;
    in his rising is our hope;
    in his gift is our power.
We thank you for sending us your Son
    and for his gift of the Holy Spirit.

Father,
    we pray for the hungry of the world;
        for mothers distressed by lack of food for the family;

for fathers too weak to work or to walk;
for children, famished to the point of death.
We pray that people everywhere may learn to care,
resolve to share,
so that there is bread for the hungry,
that together we may feed the world.

Jesus,
you send us out to be witnesses
and we gladly take your message of love.
We have nothing more precious to share.
This is the bread of life,
this brings the peace that passes understanding.
So go with us, Lord,
direct our speaking and our action
that we may be worthy ambassadors for you.

THE LORD'S PRAYER

RESPONSE

L: When we come to the end of our meagre resources
R: you inspire and enable us from the abundance of your love.

May your feet walk in the way of the Lord
May your voice speak the word of the Lord
May your hands serve God in blessing others
May your life show something of the glory of God
May you know the peace of God now and always

DAY 32

Where the waves of the sea roll powerfully
Where the waves of sound come quietly
Where the waves of emotion stir deeply
We greet our Saviour in glad encounter

RESPONSORIAL PSALM: 84:10–12

L: Better is one day in your courts than a thousand elsewhere;
R: I would rather be a doorkeeper in the house of my God
than dwell in the tents of the wicked.

L: For the Lord God is a sun and shield;
R: the Lord bestows favour and honour;

L: no good thing does he withhold
from those whose walk is blameless.
R: O Lord Almighty, blessed is the man who trusts in you.

READING: Acts 1:12–26

MEDITATION

The apostles were together in prayer. In what shall we find our togetherness, our unity of mind and heart? In our churches we strive for unity but so often division takes over. In our national life there is division and inequality. In family life dissension can easily undermine our well-being. In our local community what differences are there in priority and purpose, what tensions lie beneath the surface? The apostles were individuals. No doubt they were divided in many opinions. But they were at one in fundamental purpose and they came together in prayer; they sought the guidance of the Holy Spirit in matters of importance, like seeking a successor in the apostolate. As Christians today, we face great opportunities. There is a mission field all around us. There is wide scope for service to be offered in Christ's name. But to be effective in mission and in service we need to be a people of prayer and we need to be united in heart and mind.

'They all joined together constantly in prayer.' (1:14)

PRAYERS

Lord Jesus,
you called together a team of people to be your disciples,
varied in their character, gifts and talents.
When one failed you, another was chosen to fill his place.
So you have chosen us to do your work;
you have an intention for us.
If we fail you, another will take our place.
Help us to be faithful to your commission;
make us loyal disciples ready to follow you.
When we fall short, help us to start again,
renewed for service and for mission.

Father,
we hold before you the children of the world;
homeless children where families are refugees;
hungry children in places that experience famine;
battered children from broken homes;
neglected children in inner-city areas;
lonely children in remote parts of the country;
orphaned children in places of violent conflict.
As Jesus blessed the children long ago
give your blessing to the children of today
and help us to care for them as precious gifts.

Holy Spirit,
your gifts are wonderful and we thank you for them.
We thank you for the gift of healing.
How good it is to see sick people made well,
to witness the blind regaining sight
and the lame being able to walk.
We thank you for those engaged in medical research,
for doctors, nurses and surgeons.
We thank you for all those with a ministry of healing
and all who express your gift of healing.

RESPONSE

L: When we come to you in faith, Lord God,
R: you hear and answer with wisdom and with love.

May the Lord of the silver moon shine upon you
May the King of the myriad stars reign over you
May the Maker of the bright sun shed warmth around you
May the living Centre of the great Universe draw you to himself

DAY 33

In the busy shopping precinct, I find the Father
In the street, above the traffic's roar, I hear the Son
In the smoke-filled club, I meet the Spirit
Blessed Three, present in human company

RESPONSORIAL PSALM: 85:8–11

L: I will listen to what God the Lord will say;
R: he promises peace to his people, his saints –
      but let them not return to folly.

L: Surely his salvation is near those who fear him,
R: that his glory may dwell in our land.

L: Love and faithfulness meet together;
      righteousness and peace kiss each other.
R: Faithfulness springs forth from the earth,
      and righteousness looks down from heaven.

READING: Acts 2:1–24

MEDITATION

The day of Pentecost was exuberant, uninhibited, like the jar of perfume which Mary poured out so liberally. We tend to be much more restrained in our worship, in our offerings and in our witness. But there are times for letting go, for allowing the Holy Spirit to take over. There are times for seeing visions and dreaming dreams and for prophetic word and action.

Such a time is this one. When fear mounts, despair is rampant, defences are built and aggression is expressed. Now is a time to dream of a better world, to have a vision of a transformed society. And the vision has to be earthed in places where people suffer and struggle. We live in days which could so easily culminate in terror and destruction, in blood and fire. But equally it could be a time for the pouring out of the Spirit, of signs and wonders, and the turning of minds and hearts to God. The inspiration for making our days a time of reconciliation and peace is found in Jesus of Nazareth, a man accredited by God in his ministry of miracles and wonders. Through him all things are possible; he commissions us to be his witnesses and his peacemakers.

" '*Jesus of Nazareth was a man accredited by God to you by miracles, wonders and signs.*' '
(2:22)

PRAYERS

Lord of love,
   help us in our youth to see visions
      and in our old age to dream dreams.
   You created us to live in harmony
      and to be at peace with our neighbour.
   Help us to work for a world of caring and sharing;
      grant us in our day the joy of signs and wonders
      and of seeing your kingdom established.

God of light,
  we hold before you the homeless of the world;
    the refugees who have fled from violence and oppression;
    those living in cardboard shacks in Asia;
    those living in shop doorways in Europe;
    those driven from villages in Africa by famine;
    those who have no home in our own town
    or who live in conditions unfit to be called home.
  Be with them to comfort and strengthen them,
    to bring light into dark places,
      and inspire us to make a common effort
    that the homeless may be housed
      and the humble lifted up.

Loving Saviour,
  we are witnesses that you were raised to life
    and that in your resurrection is our hope.
  You did not abandon your people;
    you accepted suffering and death on the cross
    to give us the hope of life.
  Be with us as we announce that good news
    to all who long to hear.

RESPONSE
  L: Creator God, when despair threatens to overtake your people
  R: help us to respond with vision and to act with compassion.

May the God of travellers be with you as you journey
May the Christ of the pilgrim way walk alongside you
May the Spirit of light illumine your path
Go well and the God of peace go with you

In the face of the oppressed I hear the voice of God
In the face of the brutalised I see the face of Christ
In the bitterness of the prison camp I encounter the Spirit
Holy Trinity, at one with people suffering,
transforming, liberating, enlivening

RESPONSORIAL PSALM: 86:3–6

L: Have mercy on me, O Lord,
          for I call to you all day long.

R: Bring joy to your servant,
          for to you, O Lord, I lift up my soul.

L: You are kind and forgiving, O Lord,
          abounding in love to all who call to you.

R: Hear my prayer, O Lord;
          listen to my cry for mercy.

READING: Acts 2:37–47

MEDITATION

What a lovely picture of the simple and sincere life of those early Christians. They met for worship in the temple but they also consecrated their homes for the worship of God. In the breaking of bread they recalled the broken body of their Lord. They were a praying people, a singing people, a joyful people and they knew themselves to be a people of promise.

And what of us? We have inherited those promises. We know that if we believe, putting our trust in God through Christ, we shall be forgiven and we shall receive the gift of the Spirit. Do we worship God with gladness in our church and in our home? Do we offer our homes and our resources for the mission of the church? Do we understand that the promise is to our children too? Do we encourage our children to follow in the faith? Do we share with one another and care for one another and see signs and wonders in our life together? The early church grew because the believers made a simple and joyful witness to the faith. We too will see the church growing around us if we offer our lives, our churches, our homes, to God for his glory.

'They broke bread in their homes and ate together with glad and sincere hearts.' (2:46)

PRAYERS

Lord our God,
     you call us and you send us;
          we go out in the power of your Spirit
          to proclaim your word of life.
     May we know ourselves to be forgiven people.
     May we find joy in breaking bread together
          and in our prayer and worship.
     May we see the church grow in numbers,
          in depth of faith and in readiness for service.
     May we all with one heart and voice
          praise you for all your gifts of love.

Healer Jesus,
    we pray for those who are sick
        and those who endure pain and suffering.
    We hold in our hearts before you
        relatives and friends for whom we seek your help.
    You visited the villages and towns of Galilee,
        stretching out your hand to heal,
        and the people rejoiced to see signs and wonders.
    We too rejoice at the skill of doctors and nurses;
        we are amazed at the wonders of science and research.
    Yet we know too that there are those
        for whom medical skill can give no help.
    Be near, we pray, to give your healing touch
        and to strengthen and inspire those who suffer pain.

Holy Spirit,
    you come at times with flames of fire
        and the noise of a rushing wind.
    At other times you come like dew from heaven
        and quietly fill your people.
    Descend on us and create within us inner silence
        that, being a people of peace,
        we may speak peace to others.

RESPONSE

L: When we are together, united in prayer and purpose
R: the Lord God uses us for the glory of his name.

May the Creator God encircle you with his love
May Jesus our Lord encircle you with his joy
May the Holy Spirit encircle you with his peace
May the blessed Trinity fill you with hope and faith

DAY 35

In you I find all roads meet
In you I find all hope is complete
In you, Lord, the fulfilment of life's story
In you, Lord, the fullness of glory

RESPONSORIAL PSALM: 86:11–13

L: Teach me your way, O Lord,
        and I will walk in your truth;
R: give me an undivided heart,
        that I may fear your name.

L: I will praise you, O Lord my God, with all my heart;
        I will glorify your name for ever.
R: For great is your love towards me;
        you have delivered my soul from the depths of the grave.

READING: Acts 3:1–10

MEDITATION

Out of an ordinary situation something quite extraordinary takes place. They were going to church to pray and there they met a person in need. It would have been so easy for Peter and John to pass by. They had no money and the man was clearly begging. They did not pass by and they offered the man so much more than he asked for. They offered him the ability to help himself, the recovery of self-reliance. The crippled man was healed and how he jumped with delight!

So we too encounter people in the ordinary situations of life. It may be a woman or man unemployed and needing help. We can give them a hand-out to help with the immediate situation. We can offer crisis aid and no doubt they would appreciate our concern and generosity. But if we could work a miracle and give them a job so that they recovered self-reliance, then they would jump for joy. And isn't it possible, given the readiness to re-think our priorities and to use our political voice? Hope for the future may be found in the practical expression of a faith that cares.

'Then Peter said, "Silver or gold I do not have, but what I have I give you. In the name of Jesus Christ of Nazareth, walk." ' (3:6)

PRAYERS

Creator God,
    you placed a rainbow in the sky,
        a sign that never again would the waters flood the whole land.
    Help us to see that the cross is a universal sign of your love,
        assuring us that your people will not perish
        but, trusting in Christ, will find eternal life.

Dear Jesus,
    how wonderfully your disciples expressed their faith.
    They took you at your word and healed the sick;
        the crippled man walked and shouted for joy.

Grant us at the least a mustard seed of faith
    and a readiness to act
        that we too may see the miracle of grace.

Holy dove,
    brooding over the chaos before time began,
    hovering over the chaos before time ends,
        fill our lives with your peace,
        inspire us in the work of reconciliation,
        and enfold us in the love
            that binds all together in perfect harmony.

RESPONSE
L: When the sick cry out in pain and suffering
R: stretch out your hand to heal and help.

May your rising be as the lark for happiness
May your working be as the ox with contentment
May your resting be as the dove for peace
May your days and nights be surrounded by God's splendour

<table>
<tr><td>

DAY
36

</td><td>

In the desert hear the wind over the sands
In the wilderness experience the quiet over the land
In the wasteland hear the voice of God
In the wilderness experience God's presence and his peace

</td></tr>
</table>

RESPONSORIAL PSALM: 89:1–2

    L: I will sing of the Lord's great love for ever;
    R: with my mouth I will make your faithfulness known
          through all generations.

    L: I will declare that your love stands firm for ever,
    R: that you established your faithfulness in heaven itself.

READING: Acts 3:11–26

MEDITATION

    What is health? It is more than the absence of disease. It is balance, completeness, wholeness. By this standard all of us are unhealthy to some degree and need healing. Jesus gives perfect health. No half-measures in his gift. It is health of body, mind and spirit.

    There was, for example, a lady who was crippled with arthritis and also filled with many resentments. To visit her was to receive a catalogue of those who had offended her. Christian friends prayed for her healing. Over a couple of years she gradually changed. She was still housebound by arthritis but no longer bound by a negative spirit. To visit her was to be greeted with a smile and to hear her speak well of people. She was a lovelier person.

    We see around us many needs, physical, mental and spiritual. We should pray for wholeness, for God's influence in every area of life. Through faith in Jesus comes complete healing, perfect health.

' *"It is Jesus' name and the faith that comes through him that has given this complete healing to him."* ' (3:16)

PRAYERS

    God of Sarah and Abraham,
        we give you thanks for your disciples,
            for men and women who by faith
                proclaimed good news, healed the sick,
                comforted the sorrowing and gave hope to the despairing.
        Grant us the grace like them
            to testify to your love
            and to be signs of the kingdom.

    Lord of all hopefulness,
        may the nations of the world find peace;
        may the leaders of the nations seek your way of peace;
        may people live in harmony together;
        may the wise men and women of today follow the star of hope
            and put their trust in the Prince of Peace,
                Jesus, child of love.

Loving Shepherd,
   we pray for those who are social workers,
      probation officers and others who give personal service.
   May they be kind, gentle and loving in their care;
      may they be ready to offer time, energy and talents
         to help those in trouble, need or distress,
            giving people new hope and a new beginning.
   May they find inspiration in the example of Jesus,
      our Lord and Saviour.

RESPONSE

   L: Lord, where there has been a winter of despair
   R: may there be a spring of new life and new hope.

May the Father who loves you bless you
May the Son who redeems you bless you
May the Spirit who enables you bless you
May the Holy Trinity bless you this and every day

Creator God, open our ears to hear your Word
Loving Jesus, open our eyes to see your cross
Holy Spirit, open our hearts to receive your gifts
Blessed Trinity, dwell in us and may we dwell in you

RESPONSORIAL PSALM: 89:5–8

L: The heavens praise your wonders, O Lord;
R: your faithfulness too, in the assembly of the holy ones.

L: For who in the skies above can compare with the Lord?
R: Who is like the Lord among the heavenly beings?

L: In the council of the holy ones God is greatly feared;
R: he is more awesome than all who surround him.

L: O Lord God Almighty, who is like you?
R: You are mighty, O Lord, and your faithfulness surrounds you.

READING: Acts 4:1–12

MEDITATION

They were taken to prison because they proclaimed the risen Lord. They were questioned because they healed a cripple in the name of Jesus. They caused a stir and made a difference. They were ready for the cost of discipleship. They declared Jesus to be the way to salvation.

Many of us live in multicultural areas where we meet people of varied faiths. The Muslim and Hindu, the Buddhist and Sikh, have something to teach us. We should be ready to listen and will find that many have travelled far on the spiritual path. As Christians we are ready to share our experience and our faith. Jesus does not point the way but declares himself to be the Way. The key to the mystery of salvation is found in the suffering, death and resurrection of Jesus. Paul at Athens is not an exclusivist, denying the reality of the spiritual experience of those he meets. But he identifies Jesus as being the goal of their spiritual quest. In Jesus they will find the fulfilment they have longed for in seeking to come close to God. And those who have come to the heart of God will find that Jesus is with them.

' *"Salvation is found in no one else, for there is no other name under heaven given to men by which we must be saved."* ' (4:12)

PRAYERS

Lord God,
    you sent your Son Jesus into the world
        because you loved your people in all their variety
            and you long for them to have eternal life.
    May they come from the east and west, from north and south;
    may they gather, black and white, old and young;
    may they come from all nations,
        women and men, poor and rich;

may they bring their culture and gifts in rich variety,
  and at the name of Jesus may every knee bow
    and all the different tongues proclaim
      that Jesus Christ is Lord.

Jesus, teacher and preacher,
  we pray for all those who are ministers of the gospel.
  May they proclaim your word with courage and faith;
    may they serve others with humility and compassion.
  Lead them into truth as they study your word.
  Inspire them with wisdom as they preach the good news.
  In the care of their flock,
    grant them the shepherd's care and love.
  May they be people of spirituality and prayer
    and find fulfilment in the life of discipleship.
  We pray in your precious name.

Lord of all life,
  your love to me is more precious
    than the finest of wines and the most costly perfumes.
  You draw me to yourself and I am filled with joy
    to know the depth and wonder of your love.
  Surpassing all earthly gifts
    your love is precious.

RESPONSE

L: When trouble and persecution fall upon your church
R: give to your saints the faith and courage to endure.

Go into the world to speak with courage
Go into the world to act with compassion
Go into the world to encourage your neighbours
Go into the world to witness to the gospel
And may the blessed Trinity, Father, Son and Spirit,
  inform and inspire your thinking, speaking and action

DAY 38

May there be silence around us and within us
May the silence be deep and full of meaning
May the silence be profound and healing
May the silence speak to us of God

RESPONSORIAL PSALM: 89:9–13

L: You rule over the surging sea;
     when its waves mount up, you still them.

R: You crushed Rahab like one of the slain;
     with your strong arm you scattered your enemies.

L: The heavens are yours, and yours also the earth;
     you founded the world and all that is in it.

R: You created the north and the south;
     Tabor and Hermon sing for joy at your name.

L: Your arm is endued with power;

R: your hand is strong, your right hand exalted.

READING: Acts 4:13–22

MEDITATION

How can we be silent? There are those who have discovered the cost of discipleship. *More than Conquerors*, the report of an ecumenical group which visited Central America, tells the story of Donato Mendoza who was a catechist in Nicaragua. The Contras came and took him from his home. They gouged out his eyes, tore out his fingernails, broke many bones, tore strips of flesh from his legs, then shot him. His tortured body was found on Good Friday. He could have kept silent and saved his life. But what is life if we are to keep quiet about the love of God and the good news we receive from Jesus Christ? If we were silent the stones would cry out and we would have become stones for our silence. How can we be silent? How can we remain dumb when women and men are tortured? How can we be speechless when children suffer oppression? We must be a voice for the voiceless. We cannot but speak of all we have read and heard and experienced of the love of God.

' *"We cannot help speaking about what we have seen and heard."* ' (4:20)

PRAYERS

Weaver God,
    you bring together the rich tapestry of life;
        amidst the green of our jealousy and envy,
        alongside the scarlet of our passion and pride,
        amidst the warm brown of our friendships
        and the blue of our spiritual gifts
    may there always be the golden thread of your love
        and the silver thread of our response to you.

God of peace,
we pray for the country of Nicaragua
and other countries in Central America.
Where there has been division and conflict,
where there has been atrocity and killing,
may there be a new spirit of reconciliation
and a desire to establish justice and peace.
Guide and inspire all those in government
that they may seek the welfare of all the people;
may those who dissent learn to use the ballot box
rather than bombs and bullets.
May the hurts of the past be healed
and a time of national reconstruction begin.
We give thanks for the courage and faith of the martyrs
whose costly witness is a constant inspiration to the church
to proclaim in word and action the gospel of Jesus Christ.

Speak to me, lover of my soul, shepherd of the flocks.
You bring your sheep of many folds
and care for us all, knowing each by name.
You make us lie down in the noon sun;
you guide us back when we wander away.
Shepherd, lover of your sheep,
guide us back to your shepherd tents
and tend us with your shepherd's care.

THE LORD'S PRAYER

RESPONSE

L: When the forces of darkness threaten to overwhelm us
R: flood our lives with your glorious light.

May God be with you in the saying of your prayers
May God be with you in the doing of your work
May God be with you in all your time of leisure
May God's light illumine all your pilgrim way

May the Father surround me with love and care
May the Son speak to me his comforting word
May the Spirit engulf me with creative fire
Blessed Trinity, holy Three, around and within me

RESPONSORIAL PSALM: 89:14–16

L: Righteousness and justice are the foundation of your throne;
R: love and faithfulness go before you.

L: Blessed are those who have learned to acclaim you,
R: who walk in the light of your presence, O Lord.

L: They rejoice in your name all day long;
R: they exult in your righteousness.

READING: Acts 4:23–37

MEDITATION

Why do we feel the need to possess so much and to claim possessions as 'mine' regardless of the needs around us? The people of the early church expressed a true community, making a common pool from shared resources and having a mutual concern for each other's welfare. Where faith and love came together, the Spirit was mightily experienced with signs and wonders, healing and proclamation of good news with power. Where do we find such community today and where see such signs? The root has been transplanted and grown awry as in 'communism' and 'community council' where the name is no guarantee of the nature. We need to come together in common concern and, if all is not held in common, let it at least be held in stewardship. Another's needs must take priority over my possessiveness. To give and to share becomes a benediction for the people of God.

'All the believers were one in heart and mind. No one claimed that any of his possessions was his own, but they shared everything they had.' (4:32)

PRAYERS

Dear Lord and parent of us all,
   forgive our selfishness, our holding back and half-heartedness,
      our pride, our greed and our materialism.
   Make us generous in spirit, ready to share,
      not too greedy to give, not too proud to receive.
   So may we become a community of love.

Saviour of the world,
   you bring peace of mind;
   you heal our bodies of diseases;
   you free our spirits of depressions;
   you make us one with the Creator
      by your free gift of grace.
   Bring us to peace with our neighbours;

help us to work for harmony between nations.
May there be between us and our Father
the bond of peace, your Holy Spirit.

Lord,
you are to us the rose of Sharon,
the lily of the valley.
You are the apple tree in the wood
and your fruit is refreshing to us.
You give us a feast beyond our deserving
and your banner over us is love.
Sustain us with your gifts of grace
and may we respond to the beauty of your righteousness
with lives offered to you in joyful service.

RESPONSE

L: Loving Saviour, when your saints are put in prison
R: enable them to speak your word with courage and with boldness.

May the Father go with you on your journey of discovery
May the Son be your companion on your pilgrim way
May the Spirit be your guide in your quest for truth
May the blessed Trinity be with you by day and by night

Spirit break me, Spirit make me
Spirit mould me, Spirit enfold me
Spirit challenge me, Spirit comfort me
Spirit empty me, Spirit fill me

RESPONSORIAL PSALM: 90:1–2, 4
    L: Lord, you have been our dwelling-place throughout all generations.
    R: Before the mountains were born
        or you brought forth the earth and the world,
        from everlasting to everlasting you are God.

    L: For a thousand years in your sight
        are like a day that has just gone by,
    R: or like a watch in the night.

READING: Acts 5:1–11

MEDITATION
    The sin of Ananias and Sapphira was to promise more than they were prepared to give. It was not a matter of giving too little; that was for them to decide. It was the deception that was wrong. But what of us? What have we promised to God publicly and what have we held back in practice? It is so easy to deceive our neighbours, even to deceive ourselves. But we cannot lie to God. Our self-deception is discovered and we are without excuse. We have our choice to make. The principle of stewardship is that all our possessions are held in trust from God, not to be used selfishly but with concern for the needs of others. We must decide in stewardship what we give to the poor, what for the work of the church and what for our own use or pleasure. We can offer little or much to God. What we offer we should be prepared to give.

'With his wife's full knowledge he kept back part of the money for himself, but brought the rest and put it at the apostles' feet.' (5:2)

PRAYERS
    Lord,
        forgive us.
        So often we half-know what we do.
        We pretend to ourselves and to others
            that we have given all to you,
        but deep in our hearts there are reservations,
            escape clauses, options, half-promises
                never intended for redemption.
        Forgive us and accept us
            as we make a fresh and meaningful commitment
                in the name of Jesus.

    Living Lord,
        you gave your holy word to your people
            that we might know your truth.

Guide and bless all those with skills in writing;
may they seek to express what is wholesome and good;
may they write to instruct or to entertain,
   not to disgust, to tempt or to debase.
May creative writing play its proper part
   in welfare and learning for our nation.

Loving Lord,
   when I have been through a time of bitterness and despair
      you cross hills and mountains to come to me
         and you give me new hope.
   In your coming the winter is past;
      the time for singing has come
      and we hear the cooing of the doves of peace
      and blossom spreads its glory over the trees.
   Lord of love, your voice is sweet to me,
      your face is lovely.
Come quickly, Lord, come.

RESPONSE

L: God of Abraham and Sarah, when we make our promises to you
R: *help us to be faithful in keeping our vows*
      as you are in your love to us.

May the peace of the rivers be in your heart
May the peace of the trees be in your life
May the peace of the stars be in your soul
Peace of the Great Spirit to you and yours

DAY 41

Let the peace of God be woven into our hearts
Let the joy of God be woven into our minds
Let the love of God be woven into our lives
Weaver God, weave your divine pattern into our being

RESPONSORIAL PSALM: 90:13–16

L: Relent, O Lord! How long will it be?
  Have compassion on your servants.

R: Satisfy us in the morning with your unfailing love,
  that we may sing for joy and be glad all our days.

L: Make us glad for as many days as you have afflicted us,
  for as many years as we have seen trouble.

R: May your deeds be shown to your servants,
  your splendour to their children.

READING: Acts 5:17–32

MEDITATION

Happy the man or woman who finds that duty to God and duty to the State coincide. But what of the times when the State demands an action which in conscience we cannot agree to take? To accept our share of common burdens, to give part of our earnings to maintain hospitals or schools, are expressions of the gospel. But shall I yield up a Jewish neighbour to the terror of anti-Semitic tyrants? Shall I refuse sanctuary to campesinos fleeing from atrocities in Central America? Shall I be silent when Palestinians are murdered in their camps? Shall I give taxes to build missiles capable of pulverising cities with nuclear destruction? Shall I be silent in hostile environments when I am commissioned to preach the gospel? These situations may present us with a moral dilemma or crisis of conscience. Happy the man or woman who is persecuted for righteousness' sake, for theirs is the kingdom of heaven.

'Peter and the other apostles replied: "We must obey God rather than men!" ' (5:29)

PRAYERS

Lord,
  we thank you for the apostles
    who courageously witnessed to the faith
    even when it meant imprisonment and martyrdom.
  May the example of Peter,
    whose denial turned into costly affirmation,
    inspire us in our discipleship
    as we seek to follow our Lord Jesus Christ.

Holy God,
  we hold before you the martyr church in our generation;
    the saints in Southern Africa
      who stand up for justice and righteousness,
        giving thanks for those who have paid the price
          in suffering and martyrdom;

those in the Middle East
  who have experienced suffering, bombs and bullets
    and been taken hostage
      as they have sought to hold the faith;
the catechists, pastors and people
  of El Salvador, Nicaragua and Guatemala
  who have endured atrocities and seen their relatives killed.
May those who have suffered know your comfort
  and those who have been martyred have the crown of life
    in the joy of your heavenly kingdom.

Loving Lord,
  there are times when I feel lost and abandoned
    and I search for you.
I go about in the city, through its streets and squares,
  looking for you, lover of my soul.
People may see me as I come and go
  and wonder why I search, looking this way and that.
When I feel I can search no longer
  and I am tempted to despair,
you find me and draw me to yourself;
you do not let me go; you hold me.
Then I know that I am not rejected nor thought to be worthless.
Loving Lord, you welcome me back.

RESPONSE

L: Father, when persecution threatens to overwhelm your saints
R: grant them courage, endurance, faith and hope in Christ our Lord.

God be with you in your greeting of the day
God be with you in the work you undertake
God be with you in your worship of his name
God be with you in your resting through the night

<table>
<tr>
<td>

DAY
42

</td>
<td>

Make your circle around us, Creator God of the winds
Make your circle around us, loving Lord of light
Make your circle around us, holy Spirit of fire
Make your circle around us, blessed Trinity

</td>
</tr>
</table>

RESPONSORIAL PSALM: 91:1–4

L: He who dwells in the shelter of the Most High
        will rest in the shadow of the Almighty.
R: I will say of the Lord, 'He is my refuge and my fortress,
        my God, in whom I trust.'

L: Surely he will save you from the fowler's snare
        and from the deadly pestilence.
R: He will cover you with his feathers,
        and under his wings you will find refuge;
        his faithfulness will be your shield and rampart.

READING: Acts 6:1–7

MEDITATION

There is so much to do in the life of the church and the community. There are the practicalities of maintaining the buildings and raising the funds. Then there is the care of people in the multitude of their needs – housing the homeless, feeding the hungry, counselling the depressed, befriending the lonely. All these are worthwhile acts in themselves, but what of the vocation to prayer and preaching? Is there no place for study, for silence, for teaching and for proclamation? In a balanced Christian life there is time for caring and for sharing but we should remember the right demands of a particular vocation. It is good that the faith should be declared both in word and action. Here is no contradiction but a proper synthesis. Prayer and action also go hand in hand. Unless the people of God have a deep spiritual ground in which to root their lives, overactivity will simply uproot their faith. Deep-rooted faith enables spiritual fruitfulness.

' "We . . . will give our attention to prayer and the ministry of the word." ' (6:4)

PRAYERS

Servant Lord,
    you took the towel, badge of service,
        and gave your disciples an example in humility.
    We thank you for those who give service
        in church and community today.
    We pray for those who maintain church buildings,
        those who raise church funds,
        the organisers of meetings
        and all those who offer practical gifts in your service
            and in meeting needs around us.

You wept, dear Jesus, as a mother weeps for her children
    because the people of the city did not know
        the things that make for peace,
    so tragedy and destruction lay ahead of them.
You weep over our cities today, dear Lord,
    because we have yet to learn the way of peace
        and destruction still threatens our cities.
Save us, Lord, from that impending tragedy
    and lead us in the way of your peace.

When I lie awake and sleep eludes me,
    when I wonder if anybody cares in the darkness of life,
        then I hear you knocking.
You are my sister, my dove,
    and you call on me to open the door.
When I break from my reverie, escape from my misery,
    I draw back the bolts,
    I open the door to my life.
At times it seems no one is there to greet me
    and I feel doubly crushed.
But if in patience I wait and pray
    like the dawn breaking you come to me,
        my sister and my friend, lovely and loving,
    forgiving me, making me welcome,
        bringing me home, finding peace
            with the doves by the water streams.

RESPONSE

    L: When the pressures of life are intense, Lord God,
    R: may we find our rest, our inspiration and our strength in you.

Go into a world of need to give
Go into a world of hunger to share
Go into a world of despair to care
Go in love and may God go with you

I give you my time, Lord, for you give us eternity
I give you my talent, Lord, for you gave us your Son
I give you my love, Lord, for you gave us your Spirit
I give you my self, Lord, for you give us our being

RESPONSORIAL PSALM: 91:9–13

L: If you make the Most High your dwelling –
     even the Lord, who is my refuge –
R: then no harm will befall you,
     no disaster will come near your tent.

L: For he will command his angels concerning you
     to guard you in all your ways;
R: they will lift you up in their hands,
     so that you will not strike your foot against a stone.

L: You will tread upon the lion and the cobra;
R: you will trample the great lion and the serpent.

READING: Acts 6:8–15

MEDITATION

It is good to express power – not power as the world views it, but the power of God. It is satisfying to be an agent for God's wonders and signs, and when people clamour around to be healed and helped it gives a sense of fulfilment to stretch out a powerful hand.

Stephen was a man of power in the godly sense of that word. But he was also a man of grace. Here is a word that encapsulates gentleness, courtesy, beauty, holiness and love. There are those who in expressing power become addicted to sensationalism. Sometimes a healing ministry can be blighted by too much desire for drama and popularity. But in Stephen power was wedded to grace. No wonder they said that his face was like the face of an angel. In this disciple people saw the power of God and the grace of God. What an inspiration!

'Now Stephen, a man full of God's grace and power, did great wonders and miraculous signs among the people.' (6:8)

PRAYERS

Jesus,
    giver of life and hope,
        bring your light where there is darkness;
        grant your peace where there is discord;
        inspire your love where there is hate;
        give your hope where there is despair
        and may your life overcome the powers of death.

Healing God,
    around us are a multitude of people
        with a thousand ailments and illnesses.

They come depressed; they come with cancer;
  some with blindness and some with despair.
They come with addictions and scarred minds,
  with wounded memories and faint hopes.
Reach out with your power, healer God,
  and make us channels of your grace,
  to bring restoration, to heal damaged cells,
  to bring light in the darkness, to heal the memories,
  giving life and hope and health in the name of Jesus.

Dear Jesus,
  may I take you into my heart
    as you have taken me into your heart
      for your love is stronger than death;
    it burns like a blazing fire, like a mighty flame.
  Many waters cannot quench that love;
    rivers cannot wash it away.
  If anyone were to offer all the wealth of his house for that love,
    his offer would be scorned.

Shepherd Jesus,
  your love is beyond rubies;
    neither ivory nor diamonds can compare with it.
  Your love for us is radiant,
    beyond finest gold or most precious jewels.
  May I open the door of my heart to you;
    may I serve you until the day breaks and shadows flee
      and I find myself in your presence
        in the perpetual radiance of the life that never ends.

RESPONSE

L: In the stillness of the night and the busy activity by day
R: may we find in you our light, our hope and our peace.

May the rain from heaven fall upon your fields
May the sun from heaven warm your growing crops
May the wind from heaven sweep through your life
And may the Lord of heaven bless you, your family and friends

DAY 44

As the darkness ends, we bow in meditation;
  as the light breaks, we sing our adoration.
With the new dawn we voice our praise;
  in each new day, our song we raise.
God be with us this and every day;
  keep us, guide us, in the pilgrim way

RESPONSORIAL PSALM: 92:1–4

L: It is good to praise the Lord
      and make music to your name, O Most High,
R: to proclaim your love in the morning
      and your faithfulness at night,

L: to the music of the ten-stringed lyre
      and the melody of the harp.
R: For you make me glad by your deeds, O Lord;
      I sing for joy at the works of your hands.

READING: Acts 7:1–22

MEDITATION

How little we appreciate the adventure involved in responding to the will of God. Abraham left his home country and familiar surroundings to journey across hostile territory, ready to make a new life. God called him to venture into unknown ways and he was ready to respond. When the people experienced oppression in Egypt, God heard their cry and called a liberator to lead them. Moses was a person of great intellect and deep spirituality. The unusual circumstances of his boyhood and adolescence prepared him for the mighty work of deliverance planned in the wisdom and purpose of God, who controls the destiny of people and nations. Oppressors may think they wield power but, as Jesus teaches, they would have no power if God did not allow it. We should be willing to take risks in our discipleship, to embark on journeys into the unknown. God who calls us will also direct, guide and enable us. May we be ready at all times to respond to God's call to adventure into pilgrimage.

' *"Moses was educated in all the wisdom of the Egyptians and was powerful in speech and action."* ' (7:22)

PRAYERS

God of Abraham and Sarah, Moses and Miriam,
    you call your people in every generation.
    Responding to that call
      takes them into distant and dangerous places.
    May neither fear nor fantasy
      prevent us from responding with courage and vision
        to your call to us to be pilgrims today.
    May we go where you lead
      and find fulfilment in doing your will.

Creator God,
   we pray for those who live in cities,
      especially those who experience deprivation and poverty
         in run-down areas and decaying estates.
   Guide and bless decision-makers and planners
      that cities may be renewed,
         homes, hospitals and schools rebuilt.
   Strengthen and inspire those who live in the city,
      especially those who experience despair,
   that they may work together to improve their situation
      and find willing partners among both rich and poor.
   Help us to recognise the abilities and needs of all
      as we seek to re-create our cities
         as places of light and life.

   We pray for the Christian fellowship to which we belong,
      thankful for our partnership in the gospel,
         grateful for the worship and sacraments we share,
   asking, Lord God, that having begun a good work in us,
      you will bring it to completion
         in the day of Jesus Christ our Lord.

RESPONSE
   L: In all the busy activity of the city streets and supermarkets
   R: may we help one another and glorify your name.

   May your path go through the forest of joy
   May your way lead through the fields of kindness
   May your road ascend the mountains of praise
   May your pilgrimage pass by the rivers of peace

DAY 45

Holy God,
take the light of my eyes to use in your glory
take the words of my life to tell out your story
take the toil of my hands to work in your praise
take the steps of my feet to walk in your ways

RESPONSORIAL PSALM: 92:12–15

L: The righteous will flourish like a palm tree,
    they will grow like a cedar of Lebanon;
R: *planted in the house of the Lord,*
    they will flourish in the courts of our God.

L: They will still bear fruit in old age,
    they will stay fresh and green,
R: *proclaiming, 'The Lord is upright;*
    he is my Rock, and there is no wickedness in him.'

READING: Acts 7:23–34

MEDITATION

We live in days when people are often not aware of the holiness of God, nor of the holy scriptures, the holy places, nor what it means to be the holy people. Perhaps we have become too materialistic to understand the realm of the spiritual, too self-centred to focus on the 'wholly other', too petty-minded to comprehend the sublime.

Moses did not find it easy to reconcile two men in conflict, nor did he find it easy to respond to the need of an oppressed people, yearning to be free. But he had a deep sense of the holiness of God. He knew that God heard the cry of the oppressed people and that he would enable a liberator to lead the people to freedom. In the name of the holy God, Moses performed wonders. When we realise that the place where we stand is holy ground, when we learn to listen to the voice of God, then we are liberated and can help to liberate others, for then we can become channels of God's power and grace.

'Then the Lord said to him, "Take off your sandals; the place where you are standing is holy ground. I have indeed seen the oppression of my people in Egypt." ' (7:33)

PRAYERS

Most holy God,
    you hear the cry of your people,
        the poor, the hungry, the oppressed,
    and you raise up your messengers
        to lead your people out from slavery into the land of promise.
    Continue to inspire and bless those whom you call in our generation
        to lead out the people from the bitterness of oppression
            to the milk and honey of freedom.
    May they speak your word with courage
        and fill your people with hope.

Loving God,
    we pray for people who are so depressed
        or living under such pressure
            that they become addicted to drugs or alcohol.
    When lives become so empty of meaning
        that the contents of a bottle or a packet
            can undermine health and well-being,
        there is a sense of despair.
    Give to such people new hope in Christ;
    by the help of your Spirit
        may they break free of their addiction
            and find strength and encouragement
                in the fellowship of your people.

Holy Spirit,
    we pray for the church in this locality
        that you may inspire its ministers and members.
    May their love abound more and more
        as old and young, black and white,
            seek to live out the gospel.
    Give us knowledge and insight
        that we may be able to discern what is good,
        that we may seek purity in thought and word,
        that we may show the fruit of righteousness
            through Jesus Christ,
                to the praise and glory of your name.

THE LORD'S PRAYER

RESPONSE
    L: God of grace, when we become too materialistic, proud or selfish
    R: remind us of the sacrifice of your Son, Jesus Christ.

    May the Father surround you with a circle of care
    May the Son surround you with a circle of love
    May the Spirit surround you with a circle of power
    May the blessed Trinity encircle you each day

Father, I offer you my each and every thought
Jesus, I offer you my each and every word
Spirit, I offer you my each and every deed
Holy Trinity, I offer you my being

RESPONSORIAL PSALM: 94:8–12

L: Take heed, you senseless ones among the people;
R: you fools, when will you become wise?

L: Does he who implanted the ear not hear?
    Does he who formed the eye not see?
R: Does he who disciplines nations not punish?
    Does he who teaches the man lack knowledge?

L: The Lord knows the thoughts of man;
    he knows that they are futile.
R: Blessed is the man you discipline, O Lord,
    the man you teach from your law.

READING: Acts 7:44–60

MEDITATION

Stephen was a practical man, chosen to be one of the deacons. A good organiser who could see to the administration of charity, leaving the apostles free to preach the gospel. But Stephen was also a spiritual person, a visionary, inspired by Jesus, living close to God.

May God grant us financiers, administrators, builders, cleaners, committee people, organisers who have spiritual vision, who dream dreams, who live close to God and who get on with the practical tasks they are given, whatever sacrifice it may involve. If they are also, as Stephen, such inspired lay preachers, how blest shall we be. Truly the 'Order of Stephen' is one of the riches of our church. We are greatly blessed that the company of saints to which we belong has such a range of talents and such a variety of spiritual gifts.

'But Stephen, full of the Holy Spirit, looked up to heaven and saw the glory of God, and Jesus standing at the right hand of God.' (7:55)

PRAYERS

Most High God,
    you sent your prophets and they were persecuted.
    You sent your Son and they crucified him.
    You sent your apostles and they were martyred.
    In every generation we learn the cost of discipleship is great.
    You did not count the cost in saving us;
        let us not count the cost in responding to your call.

Father,
    we hold before you the disabled:
        those for whom movement is severely limited;

those who suffer pain and loneliness.
We thank you for the gifts of the disabled
    and the part they play in our common life.
We thank you for the courage of the disabled
    and their determination
        not to be imprisoned by their disability.
We pray for all those who work with them in medical and social care.
Grant them in their partnership
    the joy of overcoming disability
    and the satisfaction of making a worthy contribution
        to the life of the community.

God of our mothers and fathers,
    it is our joy to preach Jesus Christ,
        not from envy or rivalry but from goodwill.
May we always be ready,
    whether circumstances are easy or difficult,
        to proclaim Jesus with joy.
May we delight to see progress
    in the faith among our fellow members
        and fruit from our proclamation and action
            by your grace and power.
May we stand firm in the Spirit,
    living a life worthy of the gospel,
        not frightened by opposition
            and finding overflowing joy in Christ Jesus our Saviour.

RESPONSE

L: Father, when testing comes and the pilgrim way is hard
R: give us strength through your Spirit
      and inspiration through your Son.

Your love leads you into the heart of God
Your trust leads you into the light of God
Your faith leads you into the place of God
May you find your centre in the life of God

DAY 47

Lord, walk with us throughout this day
Lord, speak your word in all we say
Lord, give out your love in our love's endeavour
Lord, express your joy as we abide together

RESPONSORIAL PSALM: 96:1–3

L: Sing to the Lord a new song;
R: sing to the Lord, all the earth.

L: Sing to the Lord, praise his name;
R: proclaim his salvation day after day.

L: Declare his glory among the nations,
R: his marvellous deeds among all peoples.

READING: Acts 8:1–8

MEDITATION

We are afraid of crisis. We don't like it in our business, our family life, our church, our nation, our world or ourselves. Crisis, we feel, overwhelms us. It's like a storm and we all know how the disciples yelled when they encountered one. But need it be so? A crisis in a business can lead to a complete reassessment and restructuring that brings new success. A crisis in the church can lead to a new look at the gospel and its challenge, at the community and its needs and a re-ordering or rebuilding of the church in a more relevant way. Crisis in the nation can restore a sense of unity and crisis in the world may lead us across the bridge from conflict and war to peace and co-operation. Crisis within our family can lead to heart-searching conversations and a new understanding. Our personal crisis can overwhelm us or lead to a radical re-evaluation of where we are, who we are and where we are going. When persecution fell on the early church it became the opportunity to spread the faith. Will the crisis of our times become the missionary opportunity and lead to great joy in the city?

'Those who had been scattered preached the word wherever they went.' (8:4)

PRAYERS

Holy God of Israel,
    when your saints of old were scattered by bitter persecution
        the blood of the martyr became the seed of the church.
    May the crisis of materialism and secularism,
        of indifference and hostility,
    not overpower your church today.
    May your people respond with courage and with faith
        that the crowds may hear their words
            and see the signs of divine power
        and find that villages, towns and cities
            are transformed with joy
        through the proclamation of Jesus, the Christ.

Dear Lord,
 in the crisis of the cross
  you responded with love for all your people.
 In every crisis we face
  may we find creative opportunities to serve those around us
   and to witness to our neighbours.

Father God,
 we are encouraged because you make us one with Christ;
 we are comforted and strengthened
  because you unite us in the fellowship of the Spirit;
 we have our joy completed
  by seeking to conform our life to Christ's.
 Help us to be selfless as he was;
  to be clothed with humility
   and to look to the interest of others;
  to be one in spirit, purpose and love
   to the glory of your name.

RESPONSE

L: When the darkness of persecution threatens the life of your church
*R: help us to find inspiration in Jesus Christ
    to endure and witness as children of light.*

*May the night bring you refreshment of sleep
May the day bring you challenge in work
May your companions bring you the joy of friendship
May God give you peace in your heart*

Bless our hands, Lord, that they may bless others
Bless our voices, Lord, that they may speak for you
Bless our eyes, Lord, that they may see no evil
Bless our hearts, Lord, that we may seek all good

RESPONSORIAL PSALM: 96:7–10

L: Ascribe to the Lord, O families of nations,
     ascribe to the Lord glory and strength.
R: Ascribe to the Lord the glory due to his name;
     bring an offering and come into his courts.

L: Worship the Lord in the splendour of his holiness;
     tremble before him, all the earth.
R: Say among the nations, 'The Lord reigns.'
     The world is firmly established, it cannot be moved;
     he will judge the peoples with equity.

READING: Acts 8:9–24

MEDITATION

We cannot buy the Spirit nor can we control him. God grants his Spirit to whom he wills and great things follow. In the church today we sometimes have too complicated an idea of the Holy Spirit. We try to capture the Spirit in theology or to imprison her in creeds, but that is not the way of the Spirit for she is direct and practical.

In Samaria some followers had been baptised in the name of Jesus but had not received the Holy Spirit. Peter and John did not make a crisis of the situation, nor were they prepared to leave it as it was. They laid hands on them and they received the Spirit. As simple and direct as that. We make a mistake if we think we can be effective disciples without the Spirit. We err if we think the gift of the Spirit is our gift only or to be made a cause for pride. We cannot carry out our discipleship effectively unless we have the gifts from the Spirit appropriate for our calling. Whatever spiritual gifts we have are to be used in humility and we should seek at all times to show the fruit of the Spirit. Simply and directly the Spirit is our enabler for service and mission.

'Then Peter and John placed their hands on them, and they received the Holy Spirit.' (8:17)

PRAYERS

Creator Lord,
     send down your Holy Spirit upon your church;
     teach us your wisdom,
     enliven us in worship;
     enable us for service;
     empower us for witness;
     and may we show the fruit of the Spirit
          for the glory of your name.

Loving God,
   we pray for the mentally handicapped.
   We give thanks for the contribution they make to our life together;
      for their trust and childlike nature,
      for their curiosity and creative gifts.
   May they be welcome in our neighbourhood,
      both giving and receiving;
   by the warmth of their smiles
      may they give encouragement to many neighbours.

Lord Jesus,
   we look to you to find our inspiration.
   You have the nature of God
      yet did not demand equality with God.
   You made yourself nothing, taking the form of a servant.
   You took on our human likeness and became obedient to death,
      even to death on a cross.
   So your Father God exalted you
      and gave you the name above every name
      that at your name, Jesus, we should kneel in adoration
      and every tongue in heaven and earth
         should proclaim in joyful adoration
      that Jesus Christ is Lord
         to the glory of God the Father.

RESPONSE
   L: Holy God, when we feel weak and inadequate
            for the work of your kingdom
   R: empower and enable us by the gift of your Spirit.

Go into a world of need to speak a word of hope
Go into a world of hunger to respond with acts of love
Go into a world of thirst to offer Christ's cup of water
Live and give in the name of the Father, the Son and the Spirit

DAY 49

Be with us, Lord, as we greet the day
Be with us, Lord, as we go about our work
Be with us, Lord, in the eating of our meals
Be with us, Lord, in the saying of our prayers

RESPONSORIAL PSALM: 96:11–13

L: Let the heavens rejoice, let the earth be glad;
R: let the sea resound, and all that is in it;

L: let the fields be jubilant, and everything in them.
R: Then all the trees of the forest will sing for joy;

L: they will sing before the Lord, for he comes,
he comes to judge the earth.
R: He will judge the world in righteousness
and the peoples in his truth.

READING: Acts 8:25–40

MEDITATION

Philip is such an encouragement to us because he was so ready to respond to the Spirit's prompting and so refreshingly unorthodox in what he was ready to do. Who else would run alongside a Rolls Royce going along Whitehall, ready to jump in beside the eminent passenger when it was clear he was reading a Bible? And who else would take the opportunity offered by the Serpentine to baptise a visiting state official? We have become too prosaic in our expression of worship; we lack a sense of adventure and daring in our mission. We need to be ready to take risks in our discipleship, to learn what it means to be fools for Christ. If we always aim for safety and security, we shall miss an exciting dimension of life. If we are ready to take unusual paths in our pilgrimage of faith, we shall be given the unexpected as a joyful surprise.

'Then Philip began with that very passage of Scripture and told him the good news about Jesus.'
(8:35)

PRAYERS

Lord Jesus,
we give you thanks for calling us into discipleship.
Following you we find the joy of the unexpected
as your Holy Spirit leads us into new experiences
and along unknown paths.
Help us to be ready to adventure in service
and to find fresh ways to witness
that we may share in building your kingdom.

Creator God,
we pray for artists and sculptors.
By their skill they present beauty through paint and stone,
through clay and oil.

As you created a world of loveliness,
　　so in this small way they add to the splendour of creation
　　　by their art which you inspire.
May their artistic talents be an encouragement for us all.

Lord God,
　　you are at work in us, fulfilling our purpose.
May we work out our salvation in partnership with you.
Help us to be pure and good,
　　to shine as stars against the background of darkness.
May it be our joy to proclaim the word of life
　　to the glory of your name.

RESPONSE

L:　Carpenter of Nazareth, working wood for beauty and for usefulness,
R:　*inspire those who use brush and chisel*
　　　to create objects of art and symbols of hope.

Where there is truth, there is God's blessing of peace
Where there is justice, there is God's blessing of peace
Where there is righteousness, there is God's blessing of peace
May the peace of God be in your family, in your nation and in your heart

DAY 50

Father, guide us in our journeys
Jesus, bless us in our travels
Spirit, go with us on our pilgrimage
Holy God, blessed Three,
  be with us where we go and where we stay

RESPONSORIAL PSALM: 97:1–6

L: The Lord reigns, let the earth be glad;
    let the distant shores rejoice.
R: Clouds and thick darkness surround him;
    righteousness and justice are the foundation of his throne.

L: Fire goes before him
    and consumes his foes on every side.
R: His lightning lights up the world;
    the earth sees and trembles.

L: The mountains melt like wax before the Lord,
    before the Lord of all the earth.
R: The heavens proclaim his righteousness,
    and all the peoples see his glory.

READING: Acts 9:1–9

MEDITATION

In every age there are persecutors. But how sad that the persecutors are sometimes religious people who have become narrow, exclusive and judgemental in their religion. How sad that religion which should bear fruit in compassion, kindness and patience can be used to browbeat, imprison and torture those of different opinions.

From Jesus we learn a different way. He begins with people where they are and leads them to God. Even Saul learns that he is directing his anger against the Lord himself. So it is with the persecutors and the narrow and negative religious people of today. We need to be delivered from such judgemental attitudes and to learn to celebrate with Christ. This applies also to our approach to mission. Some missions are negative, judgmental and exclusive. Mission should be positive, sensitive and inclusive; Christ's offer of salvation and invitation to discipleship are open and universal. Mission is expressed in many ways and they include the Festival of Faith, celebrating God's love.

'He fell to the ground and heard a voice say to him, "Saul, Saul, why do you persecute me?"'
(9:4)

PRAYERS

Lord God,
  help us to be attentive to your voice.
    May we hear you when you rebuke us;
    may we hear you when you direct us;
    may we hear you when you encourage us.

Forgive us the faults and denials of the past
and keep us faithful to you in all that lies ahead.

Holy Spirit,
guide with your wisdom
those who have authority for government in our nation.
May our members of Parliament be aware of the needs
of the poor and deprived;
may their decisions improve the welfare of the whole nation;
may they seek justice and peace between nations;
may our nation find its true greatness
in compassion, righteousness and mutual care.

Dear Jesus,
you are my righteousness and in you I find my salvation.
Being one with you is my great gain;
beside the surpassing greatness
of knowing you as my Lord and Saviour
all else is loss,
and the things I lose are as so much rubbish.
The desire of my heart is to know you
and to share the fellowship of your suffering
and the power of your glorious resurrection.

RESPONSE
L: When nations are in conflict and people are oppressed
R: lead us to the way of justice and peace.

May the God who created the seas give you deep calm
May the God who created the stars give you radiant light
May the God who created people grant you many friendships
May the God who is your Father abide with you always

DAY 51

May the deep peace of God be in our hearts
May the deep peace of the Son be in our lives
May the deep peace of the Spirit be amongst us
May we share the peace of the Trinity with all around us

RESPONSORIAL PSALM: 98:1–3

L: Sing to the Lord a new song,
   for he has done marvellous things;
R: *his right hand and his holy arm*
   have worked salvation for him.

L: The Lord has made his salvation known
R: *and revealed his righteousness to the nations.*

L: He has remembered his love
   and his faithfulness to the house of Israel;
R: *all the ends of the earth have seen*
   the salvation of our God.

READING: Acts 9:10–19

MEDITATION

Chosen – yet not simply for privilege; rather for suffering and for the extension of God's kingdom. The chosen people, Israel, tended to forget that they were chosen for God's work. The church today sometimes sees its place as one of privilege. Even those who receive gifts from the Spirit sometimes make this a matter of pride or a cause of division. Narrow nationalism has been a scourge in our world and narrow denominationalism has been a weakness in the church. We need a concept of one world which will lead to sharing and to peace. We need a concept of one church, renewed for service and for mission. Saul was chosen by God, against all appearances, to be an instrument for the extension of God's kingdom. Our daily prayer should be 'Lord, make me your instrument'.

'The Lord said to Ananias, "Go! This man is my chosen instrument".' (9:15)

PRAYERS

Lord,
   make me an instrument
      to bring your good news to the poor,
      to heal the sick, to bring sight to the blind,
      to announce liberty to prisoners
         and the dawning of a new day for the oppressed.
Lord,
   make me an instrument
      whereby the harmony of your love will be divine music of comfort
         for those who are sad, suffering or in need.

Father,
   we pray for your servants in the persecuted church
      as they suffer with our Lord.

Some are attacked for speaking out for freedom
    under an oppressive regime;
some are imprisoned for standing up for justice
    under a totalitarian government;
many are persecuted for proclaiming the gospel
    in places where the words of your Son
        challenge the structures of injustice.
Grant to your persecuted people the courage to endure
    so that in prison, under threats and subject to torture,
    they may be strengthened and comforted by your Holy Spirit.

Lord,
    give us the courage to speak for you
        when truth is disregarded;
    give us the courage to speak for others
        when oppressors imprison and torture people
            who speak for freedom and for brotherhood.
    Grant us the compassion to speak words of comfort;
    grant us the commitment to go on to actions
        to remove injustice and restore the right.

Christ Jesus,
    you have already won for us the prize of eternal life.
    Let me forget all that I have put behind me
        and let me strive for what is ahead.
    I set my eyes on the goal and run the race gladly
        that I may claim in heaven
            the prize which you alone have gained.

RESPONSE

L: When the buds break out in blossom
R: we know the winter is over and spring has come.

May God give you bread to satisfy your hunger
May God give you water to quench your thirst
May God who gave his Son to offer you salvation
Grant you his Spirit to enable you to serve him

I seek my peace in you, Lord
I seek my peace in you
I find my joy in you, Lord
I find my joy in you
I give my love to you, Lord
I give my love to you

RESPONSORIAL PSALM: 98:4–6

L: Shout for joy to the Lord, all the earth,
    burst into jubilant song with music;
R: make music to the Lord with the harp,
    with the harp and the sound of singing,

L: with trumpets and the blast of the ram's horn –
R: shout for joy before the Lord, the King.

READING: Acts 9:32–43

MEDITATION

    Tabitha – or Dorcas as she is also known – is a great inspiration. She was such a practical saint. She made clothes for those in need, she helped the poor; she clearly encouraged many people. How tremendous and right that she should be restored to life and health, given back to those who relied on her.

    But Tabitha is also a problem. If she was brought back from the dead, what about so many others? Practical, good, helpful people in our own generation, having many people dependent on them. Then suddenly they are plunged into the long vigil and, in spite of the prayers of many friends, eventually die.

    There is a mystery in healing and restoration as there is in the providence of God. We can give thanks for Tabitha and for her raising from the dead. We can give thanks for the Tabithas of today, for their acts of compassion and their healing by miracles of grace. And if others are gathered into God's kingdom earlier rather than later, we can be thankful for their sharing in the suffering of Christ and for their constant inspiration.

'In Joppa there was a disciple named Tabitha . . . who was always doing good and helping the poor.' (9:36)

PRAYERS

    We rejoice, dear Lord, that your apostles
        experienced so many miracles of grace.
    They healed the sick, raised the dead
        and proclaimed good news to the poor.
    Help us to be as expectant as they were,
        to be ready to walk in faith and to pray with assurance.
    May we too preach in the power of your Spirit
        and expect new life and renewed health to follow
            to the glory of your name.

    We pray for local schools and colleges.

May those who teach and those who learn
    be a community of learning.
May thoughts and words be used for the common good,
    not abused for harm.
May what is learned be applied for the good of all,
    not used simply for personal profit or prestige.
May teaching be sound and wholesome
    and learning be part of the rich heritage of our common life.

Lord God,
    help us to follow the example of the saints,
        not putting our minds on earthly things
            but finding our citizenship in heaven.
    As fellow citizens in that kingdom
        we eagerly await our Lord and Saviour, Jesus Christ,
            who will transform us by his power
        so that our lowly bodies
            shall become as his glorious body.

THE LORD'S PRAYER

RESPONSE
    L: In every place, in every age, dear Lord,
          you bless your people with abundant gifts.
    R: *In all nations, at all times, may we be ready*
          to serve the needy and proclaim your name.

May God give you light for your pilgrim way
May God give you music on your disciple's path
May God give you guidance through the maze of decision
May the Holy Trinity inspire you with courage and with hope

DAY 53

The peace of the Father is with us
The peace of the Son is here
The peace of the Spirit is with us
The peace of the Three is here

RESPONSORIAL PSALM: 98:7–9

L: Let the sea resound, and everything in it,
    the world, and all who live in it.
R: Let the rivers clap their hands,
    let the mountains sing together for joy;

L: let them sing before the Lord,
    for he comes to judge the earth.
R: He will judge the world in righteousness
    and the peoples with equity.

READING: Acts 10:1–16

MEDITATION

In the days when amenities were segregated by law in South Africa, an Indian pastor was showing me the beach near Durban. There was a section for whites only, another for the Indians, then one for the 'coloureds' and finally the part of the beach for the blacks. Yet, he said, they all jump into the same Indian Ocean – perhaps it should be reserved for the Indians. He made the point with humour rather than bitterness, yet in his country theologians had argued that blacks were inferior to whites on biblical grounds.

Peter shared the prejudice of many of his fellow Jews against associating with Gentiles. The chosen people, inheritors of the promises made to the patriarchs, were his own people. His vision challenges that exclusivity. In the same way narrow nationalism, racial prejudice and other forms of negative discrimination are challenged by God's universal offer of salvation. Our Christian faith should lead us to challenge the evil of apartheid in South Africa; it should inspire us to challenge racism in our own society and to question other forms of discrimination too. Since God is forgiving and loving, we should seek to show forgiveness and love. We have in Christ a ministry of reconciliation.

'The voice spoke to him a second time, "Do not call anything impure that God has made clean." '
(10:15)

PRAYERS

Dear God,
    you are the parent of all your people,
        gathering your children about you
            as the mother hen gathers the chicks.
    We are one family and find our brothers and sisters
        in many lands and speaking many languages.
    May love unite us in the Lord of common concern and mutual care.

Creator God,
    we are glad to use tables and chairs
        and we pray for your blessing on furniture makers.
    We are thankful for china and cutlery
        and we pray for potters and cutlers.
    We value the mobility given by cars
        and we pray for steelworkers and car workers.
    Grant skill and craftsmanship
        to all those who work with their hands
            for the benefit and welfare of the community.
    May we who see the beauty of your creation around us
        take delight in creating objects of beauty and usefulness.

Dear Lord,
    help us to rejoice in your presence.
    This day and every day may we rejoice.
    For you are close to us
        and your presence is a benediction to us.
    Let us be gentle with others
        as you are gentle towards us.
    May we cease to be anxious and fretful
        and trust you for all things,
            coming before you with our thanks and our requests.
    So may we know in Christ Jesus your divine peace
        which passes all human comprehension.

RESPONSE
    L: When darkness deepens in the night of persecution and oppression
    R: may we wait with songs of joy for the dawn of liberation.

The peace of the deep sea calm be yours
The peace of the deep forest quiet be yours
The peace of the mystic's inner silence be yours
The peace of the blessed Three be yours
    To eternity

DAY 54

In the stillness we worship God
In the quiet we know his presence
His peace passes our understanding
In the stillness we worship God

RESPONSORIAL PSALM: 99:1–5

L: The Lord reigns, let the nations tremble;
R: he sits enthroned between the cherubim,
let the earth shake.

L: Great is the Lord in Zion;
he is exalted over all the nations.
R: Let them praise your great and awesome name –
he is holy.

L: The King is mighty, he loves justice – you have established equity;
in Jacob you have done what is just and right.
R: Exalt the Lord our God and worship at his footstool;
he is holy.

READING: Acts 10:34–48

MEDITATION

There were a lot of problems caused when Jacob made a favourite of Joseph, the son of his old age. The robe of many colours gave rise to the green of jealousy and the dreams of greatness resulted in bitter hate. The selling of Joseph into slavery led eventually to a blessing for his people by the grace of God but the ills caused by favouritism should not be forgotten.

God has no favourites. His children are black and white. They include boys and girls, men and women. Gifts are showered on people in all walks of life and no person is too humble to be used as an instrument of God's will. In our church life and community we need to recognise this principle. It is not just the educated, rich and powerful who have gifts to share. Inspiration, leadership and spiritual gifts are found in some of the least educated and poorest of those around us. All those gifts need to be given expression in our common life. The Holy Spirit falls on people of every race and nation so we belong together as we demonstrate the power and love of God.

' "I now realise how true it is that God does not show favouritism." ' (10:34)

PRAYERS

Holy Spirit,
come down as the gentle dew from heaven;
bestow your gifts far and wide.
May your healing gift be expressed in India;
may your gifts of wisdom be heard in Russia;
may your gift of prophecy continue in Nicaragua;
may your gift of teaching be used in America
and may you inspire many tongues in Africa.

112

Come down, Holy Spirit,
    that throughout the world
        we may show the fruit of love, joy and peace.

Dearest Jesus,
    you delighted to call us friends rather than servants
        and you give us an example in welcoming the stranger
            and serving people of other nations and cultures.
    We thank you for the rich variety of cultures
        in our national life and local neighbourhood.
    We pray your blessing on those recently arrived in our country;
        may they know themselves welcome;
        may they both give and receive in our life together.
    May we each open our hands and hearts
        to welcome the stranger in our midst,
        to give a home to the immigrant
        and to give sanctuary to refugees.

God of peace,
    help us to express what is true,
        to desire what is noble,
        to pursue what is right,
        to delight in that which is pure,
        to rejoice in that which is lovely
        and to seek what is admirable.
    And so doing may we find
        that you surround us with your peace day by day.

RESPONSE
    L: Lord, may we be deeply rooted in the ground of your love
    R: that we may yield a rich crop of compassion.

May the Father who made you guide you in his way
May the Son who loves you inspire you each day
May the Spirit who fills you answer your deepest prayer
May the Holy Trinity surround you with his care

DAY 55

Take away from me all anxieties
Remove from me all my cares
Help me to relax in your divine presence
Come, Holy Spirit, give us your peace

RESPONSORIAL PSALM: 100:1–3

L: Shout for joy to the Lord, all the earth.
R: Serve the Lord with gladness;
come before him with joyful songs.

L: Know that the Lord is God.
It is he who made us, and we are his;
R: we are his people, the sheep of his pasture.

READING: Acts 11:1–18

MEDITATION

God sometimes gives us very clear directions in life as on this occasion when Peter was told not to reject Gentile enquirers for they too had the opportunity to repent and accept God's offer of salvation. Being so sure of God's word, Peter could not fail to obey. It is perhaps the same with us. When God clearly indicates that we are to follow a particular course we do so gladly. But so often the direction is not so clear. There are various possibilities before us and God leaves us to work out the right course for ourselves. Some Christians assume too readily that God will guide every step of life, will grant a revelation for every occasion.

Discipleship involves not only an openness to God's guidance but also a readiness to use the skills and understanding he has given us. On those occasions we need a good knowledge of the Bible, common sense, and a readiness to decide and act in the mind and spirit of Jesus as far as we are able to discern it.

' "So then, God has granted even the Gentiles repentance unto life." ' (11:18)

PRAYERS

Lord God,
  speak to us
    that hearing your Word we may readily respond.
  Guide us through your Holy Spirit
    that we may make right decisions
      in the service of your people and the work of your kingdom.
  And when the direction is not so clear for us
    help us to speak and act from the foundation
      of a firm faith in Jesus Christ our Lord.

Holy Spirit,
    in a world of hostility and hate,
    in a time of conflict and war,
    in places of violence and enmity,

come as the gentle rain from heaven,
   converting the water of discontent into the spring of hope,
   turning enmity to friendship,
      hate to love and despair into joy.

Lord Jesus Christ,
   we rejoice in the fellowship of saints,
      giving thanks for our mutual care.
   You lead us in the way of discipleship
      and we ask that we may be content whatever it may bring;
         whether brought low or lifted up;
         whether facing plenty or hunger;
         whether in abundance or poverty;
      in all the changing circumstances of life
         may we find our joy in following you
            knowing that we can do all things in the strength you give.

RESPONSE

L: When women and men gather from many nations
R: may we join them in songs of celebration.

May the Father walk with you in the quiet of the garden
May the Son accompany you on the Emmaus road
May the Spirit be your guide on the road to Gaza
May the blessed Trinity, Father, Son and Spirit,
   be with you on your pilgrim way

DAY 56

Weave your name, O God, into my mind
Weave your power, O God, into my life
Weave your love, O God, into my heart
Weaver God, may the warp and weft of your divine nature
pattern my life for your glory

RESPONSORIAL PSALM: 100:4–5

L: Enter his gates with thanksgiving
and his courts with praise;
R: give thanks to him and praise his name.

L: For the Lord is good and his love endures for ever;
R: his faithfulness continues through all generations.

READING: Acts 11:19–30

MEDITATION

Toyohiko Kagawa was one of the great Japanese saints. A convert from Buddhism to Christianity, he rejected a life of wealth and comfort in order to follow the teaching of Jesus. In doing so, he served people in the slums of Kobe in a personal and costly way, sharing his home with the destitute. At the same time he proclaimed the good news of God's love in Christ far and wide. Many came to faith through his preaching.

His bringing together of social action and evangelistic preaching is biblical and apostolic. The early disciples preached the gospel with fervour yet also concerned themselves with helping the needy, the hungry and the poor. In Christ we care for people in all their needs, physical, mental and spiritual. The work of Christian Aid, Tear Fund, CAFOD and similar organisations is not peripheral but a central expression of Christian faith as Christ's parable of the sheep and the goats indicates. It is significant too that the spiritual gifts listed by Paul in Romans 12 include giving aid and acts of mercy. The Holy Spirit inspires evangelistic proclamation and social service. In both we demonstrate the Christian faith.

'The disciples, each according to his ability, decided to provide help for the brothers living in Judaea.' (11:29)

PRAYERS

Loving God,
you call us to serve you in a world of need.
When we feed the hungry
we offer bread to Christ in the wilderness;
when we help to sink wells for thirsty villages
we offer a cup of water to Christ on the cross.
Help us to know that our community of caring
is living out the gospel in the name of Jesus our Saviour.

God of mercy,
we come before you seeking forgiveness
because we know how much we have failed you.

You created a world of beauty; you gave your people paradise.
But we have not been good stewards of the earth which we inherited.
The rivers are polluted; the air in our cities is made impure;
   forests are felled and fertile land turned to desert;
   wild animals are hunted
     and, for pride or greed, whole species are endangered.
Help us, Lord, to take better care
   of the world you gave us to enjoy.

Lord God,
   we thank you for our partnership in the gospel
     with Christians in many countries.
May we encourage one another
     as we give and receive in the name of Christ.
When the good news is proclaimed
     people believe and join the fellowship of the church.
We thank you that the church is growing in many parts of the world
     and we ask for inspiration and spiritual gifts
       that by word and action
          we too may proclaim the kingdom.

RESPONSE

L: When the cry of the widow and orphan is heard in our land
R: may we be ready to respond with compassion and with faith.

As the grains of sand on the shore are innumerable
As the stars in the sky are myriad
As the drops in the ocean are countless
So may God bless you abundantly, day by day

In the stillness of the morning
In the quiet of the day
In the stillness of the evening
I hear the voice of God and my heart rejoices

RESPONSORIAL PSALM: 102:1–2
L: Hear my prayer, O Lord;
R: let my cry for help come to you.

L: Do not hide your face from me when I am in distress.
R: Turn your ear to me;
        when I call, answer me quickly.

READING: Acts 12:1–10

MEDITATION

You can recognize the characters, can't you? Herod, James and Peter. Or are they Hitler and Bonhoeffer? or an apartheid government ranged against Tutu, Naude and Boesak? or the Christian saints in Central America and Eastern Europe confronted by their oppressors? The result is never in doubt. Whatever the power of the oppressor, the persecuted sing the hymns of triumph. However potent the tyrant, the righteous will endure to the end. Some may be put to death and earn the martyr's crown; others may spend years in prison. But through all the afflictions the persecuted look to Jesus for inspiration and find the promised Holy Spirit enables them to keep the faith and celebrate with songs of joy. They have become an inspiration to the whole church. We must all ask how much our faith means to us and whether we are prepared for the cost of discipleship. We too should face crisis in the sure knowledge that God will sustain and guide us and enable us to make our witness with courage and with joy.

'So Peter was kept in prison, but the church was earnestly praying to God for him.' (12:5)

PRAYERS

Your people were at prayers, Lord,
    and you answered with a miracle.
Your people are at prayer
    and we should be attentive, expectant,
    ready to be surprised by a miracle,
    challenged by your word, inspired by a vision
    or empowered by the descent of your Spirit.
For when we are together at prayer
    great things come to pass.
Lord, we believe; help us to overcome our unbelief.

Spirit divine,
    your gift is peace.
Such peace we know
    when walking by the wave-lapped shore of the sea.

Such peace we know in the heart of the forest
   amidst the call of birds and crackle of twigs.
Such peace comes to us
   in the constant flow of a streaming cascade.
Such peace comes to us on the mountain top
   when the clouds are around us and the bird sweeps far below.
And such peace is there in the busy rush of the city's life
   and in the heart of the shopping centre.
Spirit divine,
   your gift is peace.

God of grace,
   help us to care for one another as you care for us.
May our gifts of compassion be a fragrant offering,
   a sacrifice acceptable and pleasing to you,
      our God and Father;
for we simply respond to your love
   which meets all our need
      through the glorious riches you grant us in Christ Jesus.

RESPONSE

   L: When the clouds of doubt gather on the distant horizon
   R: scatter them by the lightning of your word.

May the Great One who is both mother and father bless you
May the Suffering Servant who is both brother and sister bless you
May the Great Spirit who is neither male nor female bless you
The blessing of the Trinity, the Great Mystery,
   be yours now and always

<table>
<tr>
<td>

DAY
58

</td>
<td>

We come apart from bustle and noise
We turn aside from clamour and anxiety
We seek our peace in the heart of God
We find our peace, we find our peace with you, Lord

</td>
</tr>
</table>

RESPONSORIAL PSALM: 102:18–22

L: Let this be written for a future generation,
R: that a people not yet created may praise the Lord:

L: 'The Lord looked down from his sanctuary on high,
from heaven he viewed the earth,
R: to hear the groans of the prisoners
and release those condemned to death.'

L: So the name of the Lord will be declared in Zion
and his praise in Jerusalem
R: when the peoples and the kingdoms
assemble to worship the Lord.

READING: Acts 12:11–19

MEDITATION

As people we can be very strange. We pray for a miracle and then express sheer astonishment when God answers our prayers. People sometimes share in prayers for someone seriously ill and then say how sad it is that the end is so near. Yet miracles occur in every generation. Broken lives are knit together, fevers are cured, lame people walk, those who have lost their voice regain it. I have seen a number of these instances myself and on one occasion saw a young girl, blind, deaf and without speech as a result of an accident, recover sight, hearing and speech under the influence of prayer like a flower opening to the sun. I have heard the thanksgiving of a lady who came forward leaning on a zimmer frame to receive laying on of hands and prayers for healing. She wrote to tell how she had been healed and now walked for miles without pain.

There are times when the recovery is not complete. But the occasions when health is restored by prayers are numerous. We should thank God for this, as well as for the healing work of doctors and nurses. Praise God from whom all blessings flow.

'But Peter kept on knocking, and when they opened the door and saw him, they were astonished.'
(12:16)

PRAYERS

Holy God,
forgive us for the many times we fail you.
Forgive those in authority when, through pride,
they use selfishly the power entrusted to them.
Forgive us when we fail to recognise your voice,
when we pray without faith or live without assurance.
Forgive us and help us to serve you better in the future
by the help of Christ our Lord.

A child's cry becomes your voice to me;
the lined features of an aged refugee your face;
the gnarled hands of the old black worshipper
   are your hands, scarred by nails;
the warm brown eyes of the elderly victim of a mugging
   are your eyes, looking to Peter;
the cry of pain from the tortured Nicaraguan priest
   is your pain under scourging;
the shout for help of a woman suffering violence
   is your voice in the garden of Gethsemane;
and through the generations, the cries, the pain
   are your suffering of insults;
the faces and voices of the oppressed
   are the radiance of your face to me.

Lord our God,
   you do not fail your people.
You supply every need of ours from the abundance of your grace
   so richly expressed in Christ Jesus our Lord.
Help us to respond by giving praise and glory to you day by day.

RESPONSE

L: When the hard ground is broken by green shoots
         and the buds burst into blossom
*R: we know that the winter of despair is over
         and the spring of new hope is come.*

May God who made the rivers, seas and oceans bless you
May God who made the fields, the hills and mountains bless you
May God who made all creatures, wild and tame, bless you
May God, Father, Son and Spirit bless you now and always

<table>
<tr><td>

DAY

59

</td><td>

Creator God,
Thou art the peace of the dove's flight
Thou art the joy of the lark's song
Thou art the grace of the deer's run
Thou art the love of mother for son

</td></tr>
</table>

RESPONSORIAL PSALM: 103:1–4

L: Praise the Lord, O my soul;
   all my inmost being, praise his holy name.

R: Praise the Lord, O my soul,
   and forget not all his benefits.

L: He forgives all my sins
   and heals all my diseases;

R: he redeems my life from the pit
   and crowns me with love and compassion.

READING: Acts 13:1–12

MEDITATION

There are different expressions of religious practice which we see in the clash of the prophetic and the priestly in Old Testament times and of those who favoured an exclusive or an inclusive concept of Christianity in New Testament times. We see it today in the clash of the ordered and institutionalised approach and the spontaneous and pentecostal approach. In the church at Antioch we find a spiritual and prayerful life which enables the preachers to be directed by the Holy Spirit who tells them to set apart Barnabas and Saul and who guides these two on their mission. Whilst we benefit from the order and organisation of the institutional church, that must never be allowed to quench the Spirit or make the members less able to hear and respond to the direction of the Spirit. In a generation when mission is so urgent, God will raise up evangelists and prophets. The institutional church can be a vital part of that movement or stand outside it. What we witness is the spiritual equipment and enabling of the true church of Jesus Christ.

'While they were worshipping the Lord and fasting, the Holy Spirit said, "Set apart for me Barnabas and Saul for the work to which I have called them." ' (13:2)

PRAYERS

Holy Spirit,
   speak to the church today.
   Guide us in the way of truth;
   equip us for the task of service;
   enable us in the work of mission;
   use us in the work of the kingdom;
   spend us in discipleship to Jesus Christ
   and help us to do all that is committed to us
      for the glory of God our Father.

122

In my inner ear I hear you speak;
    with my inner eye I see your face;
        with my inward step I follow you;
            in my inner heart I welcome you.
Christ be in me, all around me,
    walking with me, talking with me;
Christ holding me, Christ assuring me,
    my joy, my peace, my crown.

Dear Lord,
    it is our joy and privilege to be numbered with the saints.
We greet each other as sisters and brothers
    and delight that we are one family
        looking to you, our Saviour and Lord.
Be with us in our pilgrimage of faith.

THE LORD'S PRAYER

RESPONSE

L: From the dawn of each new morning to the shade of evening
R: may we seek to walk with God and to do his will.

Let the streets of the city be filled with joy
Let the houses of the city echo with praise
Let the people of the city show love to one another
May the city be a place of peace and that peace be yours always

DAY 60

In the heart of the leaf, veins
In the flat of the palms, veins
Through the veins, life blood
Drawn from heart or roots, sustenance
Given from the source of all creation
Life blood, life food

RESPONSORIAL PSALM: 103:8, 10–12

L: The Lord is compassionate and gracious,
      slow to anger, abounding in love.
R: He does not treat us as our sins deserve
      or repay us according to our iniquities.

L: For as high as the heavens are above the earth,
      so great is his love for those who fear him;
R: as far as the east is from the west,
      so far has he removed our transgressions from us.

READING: Acts 13:13–33

MEDITATION

      With the full cycle of the years the time for deliverance came and God sent his Son to be the Saviour of the world. In every generation since, the most important news for Jews and Gentiles has been this message of salvation. When Jesus came, the world was in a mess. There was violence, cruelty and suffering. Spiritual seekers were looking for redemption, a way of salvation. Today the world is in a grim situation too. Cruelty and oppression are as horrific as in any previous generation; by technological advance the capacity for destruction has reached a proportion which makes world destruction a real possibility. Ancient religions and many new sects proclaim various paths to salvation and in some cases are caught up in the cycle of violence which surrounds us. These are days to pray with the early church, 'Come, Lord Jesus.' Perhaps the intensity of suffering indicates a culmination in world history and God's purpose. Of this we can be sure. People today, of all nationalities and races, need to hear good news and it is summed up here – for all of us, this message of salvation has been sent. God's promise of redemption is fulfilled in Jesus who by his sacrifice seeks to draw all people to God. This is the news – let us seek to share it.

' *"It is to us that this message of salvation has been sent." '* (13:26)

PRAYERS

      Dear Lord God,
          you are to us both mother and father, brother and sister,
              in your loving care and deep compassion.
          You care for us even when we feel we are not worth caring about.
          In sending your Son, Jesus, you gave us a message of encouragement.
          He is your Word, the fulfilment of your promise;
              in his dying and rising we are offered new life.
          As we have been so richly blessed

help us to proclaim to others this message of encouragement
   that we may celebrate together the good news of your love.

I hold your invitation in my hand, dear Jesus,
   I keep your promise in my heart.
You know my needs; you hear my cry.
You accept the offer of my life;
   you bless the future as you blessed the past.
In this I find my constant joy and lasting peace
   that you are with me always, this day and to the end of time,
      and will be with me in the joy of heaven.

As we celebrate in worshipping our Creator
   we remember with joy our partners in the gospel.
We find our incentive to love others
   in the love of Jesus our Saviour.
We experience in God the peace that passes understanding,
   the peace too deep for words.
Knowing ourselves to be surrounded by a great crowd of witnesses,
   the saints in every age,
we pray that the grace of the Lord Jesus Christ may be with us all.

RESPONSE

L: From birth to death, in all the changing scenes and circumstances
*R: holy God, you bless us abundantly
      from the exceeding greatness of your love in Christ.*

Be still and wait on God
May the silence of the Creator enfold you
May the silence of the Redeemer surround you
May the silence of the Comforter encircle you
May the silence of the blessed Three surround you to eternity

PRAYERS
FOR PILGRIMS

Readings from Ephesians. Sometimes referred to as 'the Queen of the Epistles', this letter, with its deep theological truths and sonorous phrases, has as much challenge and encouragement for the church today as it had for the church at Ephesus.

DAY 61

God is praised by the whole of creation
  By the tiniest plant drawing sustenance from the earth
  By the smallest leaf drawing energy from the sun
  By the most minute tendril passing moisture to the fruit
    God's name is praised

RESPONSORIAL PSALM: 103:15–18

L: As for man, his days are like grass,
     he flourishes like a flower of the field;
R: the wind blows over it and it is gone,
     and its place remembers it no more.

L: But from everlasting to everlasting
     the Lord's love is with those who fear him,
     and his righteousness with their children's children –
R: with those who keep his covenant
     and remember to obey his precepts.

READING: Ephesians 1:1–2

MEDITATION

  Paul is bound to God through whom he receives his apostolate of Christ. He is also bound to God's people at Ephesus because they are one in the Lord, one in their calling, one in their worship.
  Paul greets the church at Ephesus and doing so prays a great blessing for them, expressed in the two words, grace and peace.
  Grace – a gentleness, spirituality in character, closeness to God, winsomeness in relationship.
  Peace – shalom which is health, welfare, salvation, peace, wholeness; a completeness in physical, mental and spiritual well-being.
  May Paul's prayer be for us too – grace and peace – from God our Father and Jesus our Lord.

'Grace and peace.' (1:2)

PRAYERS

  Holy God,
    you call your people in every generation
      to put their trust in you
        and to venture forward in spiritual discovery.
    We give you thanks
      that you send us out as followers of Jesus Christ
        to serve those in need and to proclaim good news.
      Give us your grace in our discipleship
        and may we find peace in your service.

  Healing God,
    we pray for those who are ill;
      especially those suffering from muscular diseases

which sap them of energy,
restrict them in movement
and cause great pain.
Give them the reassurance of your presence
and the help of many friends.
Guide all those researching the cause of such diseases
and seeking a cure.
Stretch out your hand to guide, to bless,
to help and heal.

In the one is found my unity;
in the two is bound my relativity;
in the three is made community.
Three in one, profoundest mystery,
bring me to the heart of your triune being.

RESPONSE

L: Your love for us is freely offered by your grace.
R: Help us to respond without counting the cost.

May the pillar of fire that led the Israelites be your guide
May the star that shone over Bethlehem be your guide
May the voice that spoke to Samuel be your guide
May the voice that challenged Paul be your guide
May the living God be your companion through all your days

DAY 62

May you know the blessing of rain from heaven
May the furrows of the fields be full of water
May the streams of the land never run dry
May the rivers flow majestically to the sea

RESPONSORIAL PSALM: 103:19–22

L: The Lord has established his throne in heaven,
   and his kingdom rules over all.
R: Praise the Lord, you his angels,
   you mighty ones who do his bidding, who obey his word.

L: Praise the Lord, all his heavenly hosts,
   you his servants who do his will.
R: Praise the Lord, all his works everywhere in his dominion.
   Praise the Lord, O my soul.

READING: Ephesians 1:3–6

MEDITATION

God in his giving is abundant beyond our imagining. He gives us in Christ
every spiritual gift. We are a people of immense blessing.

And we are chosen people. Chosen from the beginning of time. This is a
sublime thought. We are selected outside time, yet for a particular time. We are
part of the divine purpose, intended to be pure, to be loving, to be God's children
through Christ.

In Jesus we receive so many spiritual blessings, among which are forgiveness
and release from the slavery and hurts of the past. All of this is the free gift of
God. Nothing we do earns our freedom. It is God's abundant gift, freely offered,
through Jesus the Prince of love.

'He chose us in him.' (1:4)

PRAYERS

God and Father of our Lord Jesus,
   we give you praise for all the blessings you bestow upon us,
      especially your spiritual gifts.
   Your divine purpose is being worked out in our world;
      you chose us in Christ to be your servants;
      you chose us before time began to live holy lives.
   Since our destiny is to be adopted
         as your sons and daughters through Jesus
      help us to fulfil your purpose,
         living to the glory of your name.

Divine Architect,
   we praise you for the wonder of creation,
      for sun and moon and stars.
   We hold before you those explorers
      who have searched out paths to the planets;

130

give courage and faith to those astronauts
who have journeyed to the moon
and faced danger in far places.
Give skill and understanding
to those who design and build rockets.
As we widen our knowledge of the universe
may we deepen our knowledge of you.

In the silence I hear you speaking, holy Lord;
in the quiet I know your being, righteous Creator.
Being silent, I can hear others;
in the silence we enter deep communion.
When words cease and noise abates,
in the quiet is my renewing;
in the silence I abide in you.

RESPONSE

L: Lord God, there is no glory like the glory of your presence,
no brightness to compare with the light of your being;
R: *so fill us with the peace that passes understanding*
and enrich us with the joy that is beyond expression.

May the insects in the soil speak to you of God
May the fish in the sea speak to you of God
May the birds of the air speak to you of God
May the cattle in the fields speak to you of God

DAY 63

Amethyst, blue as the colour of the ocean
Emerald, green as the grass in the fields
Garnet, red as blood freely shed
Gems of the earth, precious,
    but not as precious as the love of God in Christ

RESPONSORIAL PSALM: 105:1–4

L: Give thanks to the Lord, call on his name;
    make known among the nations what he has done.
R: Sing to him, sing praise to him;
    tell of all his wonderful acts.

L: Glory in his holy name;
    let the hearts of those who seek the Lord rejoice.
R: Look to the Lord and his strength;
    seek his face always.

READING: Ephesians 1:7–10

MEDITATION

We are the failures, but God is faithful.
We fall short; God never misses the mark.
His love reaches out to us where we are;
    for our sake in Christ God becomes vulnerable;
in Christ he pays the price of our sins.
We are bought at a great price;
Christ's blood streams through time and eternity
    since his sacrifice is for ever.
Here is a secret, but an open secret;
    here is a mystery, but one to be unlocked.

This is God's great purpose, to free us from the shackles that bind us, and to unite us to himself in a bond of love, one God, one people, one universe, united through sacrifice, held together in love. The whole universe is to be brought together in harmony through Christ. What a tremendous consummation of world history. A planet at peace; a reconciled universe; a people in harmony with each other and all creation.

'He made known to us the mystery of his will.' (1:9)

PRAYERS

There are times, Lord God, when I know I have failed you.
You do not forsake me; in Christ you offer me forgiveness.
    Through his blood we are cleansed;
        he has bought us back at a great price.
Truly you bless us abundantly, far beyond our deserving.
You are working out your purpose
    as all history moves to a great culmination
        when you will bring all things in heaven and earth
            together in Christ.

132

Holy Lord of creation,
  Your voice is heard in the sound of many waters;
    your voice is heard in the call of many birds.
We give you thanks for music and musicians;
    for those whose composition is an inspiration;
    for those whose playing on instruments is a delight;
    for those whose voices in song
      bring a new dimension into the lives of listeners.
May those blessed with such gifts
    use them for the common good.
May they not misuse that gift for monetary gain
    or for propaganda in an evil cause.
Rather may they express harmony,
    contribute to peace in our world
      and give praise to you.

Jesus,
  you were so right;
  my eyesight is so good at seeing the speck in my neighbour's eye,
    so bad at noticing the plank in my own;
  my hearing is so good at hearing my neighbour's shameful words,
    so deaf to my own hurtful gossip.
  I can be such a clear witness to the rules broken by another
    but so lacking clarity in my own wrongdoing.
  Give to each of us a great humility
    and readiness to acknowledge our own failings
    and a greater sensitivity and willingness to forgive
      the mistakes and failings of our neighbours.

RESPONSE

L: In poverty or riches, in health or sickness,
      in freedom or in servitude,
R: it is our joy to sing your praise and to walk in your way.

May the Father, Creator of the Universe, bless you in the morning of life
May the Son, Prince of Peace, bless you in the noon of discipleship
May the Spirit, Enabler and Comforter, bless you in the evening of your days
May the blessed Trinity be with you at the rising of the sun and at its going down

DAY 64

May the wind in your face refresh you
May the sun overhead warm you
May the stars at night guide you
May the clouds in the sky be signs of God's glory

RESPONSORIAL PSALM: 106:1–3

L: Praise the Lord.
    Give thanks to the Lord, for he is good;
R: *his love endures for ever.*

L: Who can proclaim the mighty acts of the Lord
    or fully declare his praise?
R: *Blessed are they who maintain justice,*
    who constantly do what is right.

READING: Ephesians 1:11–14

MEDITATION

In Christ we receive our inheritance
In Christ we set our hope
Through Christ we praise God
Through Christ we hear the truth
In Christ we have salvation
In Christ we are sealed with the Holy Spirit
Through the Spirit we enter into our inheritance
Through the Spirit we carry out our discipleship
By the grace of God we enter eternal life.

This is our destiny; in this we find our fulfilment. The guarantee of all we are
promised is the Holy Spirit. Since we have received the gift of the Holy Spirit
we know that we shall enter the kingdom of heaven through Christ. This is our
good news; we delight to share it with others.

'The gospel of your salvation.' (1:13)

PRAYERS

Holy God,
    we give you praise that we have heard the word of truth;
        that we have received the good news of salvation.
    You have chosen us in Christ
        and through him our hope does not fail.
    We give you thanks that through Christ
        we have received the promised Holy Spirit
            who is our guarantee of future bliss,
                our inheritance by the same Jesus Christ.

God of peace,
    we pray for the nation of Namibia.
    Where there has been drought and hunger
        may there be refreshing streams and plentiful food.

Where there has been discrimination
    may there be racial harmony.
Where there has been war and violence
    may there be peace and reconciliation.
In a country of rich resources
    may this independent nation
    be a place of shared concern
        and mutual effort for the welfare of all its people.

There have been many occasions, Lord, of too many words.
    Your disciples argued about who was greatest;
    the Pharisees argued about sabbath observance;
    the upholders of the law were quick to condemn
        the woman taken in adultery.
We confess, Lord, that we have spoken too much;
    help us to pause, to draw lines in the sand;
    help us to pause, to put on the moccasins of others;
    help us to be silent, that we may hear.
And when we speak,
    help us to be sons and daughters of encouragement.

RESPONSE

L: In the light of each new morning,
      by the bright hope of every day
R: you fill us with joy in living
      and with happiness in achievement.

The blessing of the One be with you in your solitude
The blessing of the Three be with you in community
The blessing of the Creator refresh you in your discipleship
The blessing of Father, Son and Spirit
  keep you in the communion of saints

Grass bending with the strength of the wind
Trees leaning over before the gale
Clouds scudding across the sky before the force of the storm
God of creation, Lord of the skies, be with us

RESPONSORIAL PSALM: 107:1, 29–32

L: Give thanks to the Lord, for he is good;
R: his love endures for ever.

L: He stilled the storm to a whisper;
        the waves of the sea were hushed.
R: They were glad when it grew calm,
        and he guided them to their desired haven.

L: Let them give thanks to the Lord for his unfailing love
        and his wonderful deeds for men.
R: Let them exalt him in the assembly of the people
        and praise him in the council of the elders.

READING: Ephesians 1:15–23

MEDITATION

Let these words speak to you and to your congregation:
Your faith is heard of by the worldwide church;
The love you show to God's people is an inspiration;
You are prayed for in many places
    where they give thanks for your work and witness.
May Christ give you wisdom and vision
With your inner eyes may you see his light
May your hope never fail
May you enter into your great spiritual inheritance
May you tap the vast resources of divine power
May God who raised Christ and exalted him
    work mightily in you and through you
May God who subjected all things to Christ
    make you one with him in the fellowship of the Church.

'His incomparably great power.' (1:19)

PRAYERS

Great indeed, glorious Father, is your great power
    and incomparably wonderful your love for your people.
You enable us by your mighty power
    so that we witness not in our weakness
        but in your great strength.
Your power raised Jesus from the dead
    and set him at your right hand.
In that same power you send us out
    to heal the sick, to serve the needy
    and to proclaim good news to the poor.

Holy God,
   we pray for those who entertain us as actors and actresses.
   By the films and plays we see
      we are challenged, inspired, helped and guided.
   Sometimes we are made afraid or sad;
      often we are amused and comforted.
   May the actors and actresses
      carry out their creative work with dedication,
         never demeaning their act or debasing their activity
      but giving glory to you in characters well-presented
         to instruct and entertain.

Loving Saviour,
   we recall with thanksgiving the spiritual quest of Nicodemus
      who came to you by night seeking the way of life.
   You taught him that every person needs a spiritual rebirth,
      being born of water and the Spirit.
   We too seek to know the spiritual path.
      As we have reeived the waters of baptism
      so also being baptised in the Holy Spirit
         may we be endowed with gifts of the Spirit
      and show the fruit of the Spirit
      to the glory of God our Father.

RESPONSE

   L: Lord God, when hopes are unfulfilled and friends fail us
   R: you are always near to comfort and encourage us.

May you be blessed by the God of Moses
   who witnessed with awe the burning bush
May you be blessed by the God of Moses
   who spoke with courage God's word to Pharaoh
May you be blessed by the God of Moses
   who led his people to the Promised Land

The flower bursts through hard ground to grow towards the light
The wheat grows steadily towards the warming sun
The tree reaches its branches ever higher towards the sky
So in our life of prayer we stretch expectantly up towards God

RESPONSORIAL PSALM: 108:1–5

L: My heart is steadfast, O God;
   I will sing and make music with all my soul.
R: Awake, harp and lyre!
   I will awaken the dawn.

L: I will praise you, O Lord, among the nations;
R: I will sing of you among the peoples.

L: For great is your love, higher than the heavens;
   your faithfulness reaches to the skies.
R: Be exalted, O God, above the heavens,
   and let your glory be over all the earth.

READING: Ephesians 2:1–7

MEDITATION

We choose the way of life or of death. Many choose death, urged on by negative spirits of our generation, preferring passion, lust and violence. The descent on that path leads to extinction. But God in his great love seeks to pluck us from death and make us live again with Christ. Though we choose the way of death by our wrongdoing, God raises us with Christ to sit with him in the heavenly kingdom. This is love indeed which can bring us from being so low to attain such heights. Yet still the choice is ours – to accept or to refuse the way to life.

'Alive with Christ.' (2:5)

PRAYERS

Lord God,
   your great love for us never fails;
   when we were dead in wrongdoing,
      you made us alive in Christ.
   There is nothing we have done of which we can boast;
   rather it is by your grace so freely bestowed on us
      that we are saved by faith in Christ.
   Thanks be to you, my dear Lord,
      for gifts so incomparably rich in mercy.

Healer Jesus,
   we pray for all who suffer in body or mind,
      especially for those who experience nervous disorders
         which cause them to feel despair by day,
         to have terrifying dreams at night
         and to question whether they can cope with the future.

Place your hand in their hand.
Give them help by your grace
    and healing by your power.
Guide and enable all those who care for such sufferers
        that they may be people of compassion and patience
            who use the right methods
                to encourage recovery and health.

Creator,
    we thank you for a world of such varied loveliness;
        sun rays reflected in shining icicles
            and in the mirror ice on the lake;
        snow drifted deep in the hillsides
            and making a white tracery on the branches of trees.
    This is the winter wonder of snowflakes and ice.
    This is the beauty of your creation, Lord of the snow.
    We thank you for a planet of such great loveliness.

THE LORD'S PRAYER

RESPONSE

    L: There are times when we feel lonely even amongst a crowd of people.
    R: But you, Lord, never forsake us;
        you remain faithful through the years of our journey.

    May the sun shed its radiance upon you
    May the breezes blow freshly around you
    May showers of abundant rain fall upon you
    May the Holy Trinity bless you day by day

DAY 67

The brown twigs are clothed with light green leaves; it is spring
The light green changes to deep green; it is summer
The green turns to golden brown; it is autumn
The leaves fall, the branches are bare; it is winter
Through all the changing seasons God's sap of life flows through us

RESPONSORIAL PSALM: 111:1–4

L: Praise the Lord.
     I will extol the Lord with all my heart
     in the council of the upright and in the assembly.

R: Great are the works of the Lord;
     they are pondered by all who delight in them.

L: Glorious and majestic are his deeds,
     and his righteousness endures for ever.

R: He has caused his wonders to be remembered;
     the Lord is gracious and compassionate.

READING: Ephesians 2:8–10

MEDITATION

In the life of faith there is thesis, antithesis and synthesis. All is in God's hands, held together in his sovereign purpose. By God's good grace we experience salvation. Ours but to put our faith in him. Yet God has made us; we are his handiwork, and his purpose for us includes our working for what is good, pure and just. So we are called to good works and these are part of God's eternal purpose. Yet our salvation does not come from good works but by faith in God's ultimate and loving grace.

'Saved, through faith.' (2:8)

PRAYERS

Lord God,
    we are your creation, made by you for good works;
      let us then set our hands to what is good.
    We are your workmanship, created to fulfil your purpose;
      let us then make ourselves available in your kingdom.
    We offer ourselves to you, rough-hewn as we are;
      reshape us; finely mould us;
    may our new being proclaim your glory,
      through Jesus Christ our Saviour.

Lord of the universe,
    we pray for those whose work is the study of your creation.
    Guide the astronomers who name the stars
      and measure their distance from the earth
        and plot the course of the planets.
    May the wonders they see through their telescopes
      give them a deep sense of awe
        as they meditate on your creation.

New shoots push through hardened earth;
    branches gain a dress of green and burst into blossom colour.
The call of the cuckoo welcomes the spring
    as winter is ended and water cascades from the hills.
Animals skip with delight, released from their hibernation
    and cities after the stress of winter delight in the spring.
Lord of all the changing seasons,
    we give you thanks for the freshness and colour of spring.

RESPONSE

L: Lord God, the birds of the air, the fish of the sea
       and the animals of the field all proclaim your praise.

*R: The whole of creation, sun, moon and stars and all on planet earth
       unite in a song of adoration to give glory to you.*

*May you be blessed with courage like Abraham
    as you take your journey of faith
May you be blessed with vision like Jacob
    when he saw the ladder from earth to heaven
May you be blessed with wisdom like Joseph
    who became a blessing for his people
May you be blessed by God, creator of heaven and earth*

DAY 68

The soil, rich in texture, holding water, sustains the roots;
the roots, reaching out, drawing food and drink, sustain the stem;
the stem, drawing from the roots, sustains the branches.
The whole plant, root, stem and branches,
  gives glory to God the Creator

RESPONSORIAL PSALM: 112:4–6
> L: Even in darkness light dawns for the upright,
> *R: for the gracious and compassionate and righteous man.*

> L: Good will come to him who is generous and lends freely,
> *R: who conducts his affairs with justice.*

> L: Surely he will never be shaken;
> *R: a righteous man will be remembered for ever.*

READING: Ephesians 2:11–22

MEDITATION
> Without Christ, what are we?
> a people alienated from God, a nation without promises;
> a people without hope, abandoned.
> With Christ, what do we become?
>   a people close to God;
>   a people who have found peace;
>   a people reconciled to God and to each other.
> How is this transformation brought about?
>   By Christ, who is our peace;
>   who breaks down barriers and surpasses laws,
>   bringing us to wider harmony through the cross.
>   This is the proclamation of true peace
>   to people of all times and all places
>   by Christ brought to the Father through the Spirit.
>   Truly then in Christ
>   we stand alongside the saints,
>   we build on the foundation of the apostles,
>   we become a dwelling-place of the Holy Spirit.

'Making peace.' (2:15)

PRAYERS
> Lord Jesus Christ,
>   you are our peace;
>   when hostility divides us from neighbours,
>   when division spoils our friendships,
>   when enmity stands between nations,
>   you break down the barriers,
>   you unite us.

142

By your cross you reconcile us to God
    and bring us into harmony with each other.
Lord Jesus,
    you are our peace.

Holy Lord,
    you have created us to live together
        in mutual care as a family of nations.
    We pray for all those in positions of leadership
        in the countries of the world.
    We pray especially for political leaders
        that they may be men and women of mature judgement,
            of high ethical standards and social commitment.
    Endow them with wisdom and understanding
        that we may be led in ways of peace
            and may seek to establish justice
                in all the nations of the world.

Summer days, hot and lazy, with the murmur of bees
    and the varied calls of myriad birds,
    and crops resplendent in the fields
    and farmers busy about their tasks.
Streams have run dry; heathlands burnt black;
    but the dogrose in the hedgerows is a delight
    and the blackbirds are busy around the thickets.
Thank you, God of heaven and earth,
    for the beauty and warmth of summer.

RESPONSE

    L: Lord, when we walk with your saints in the pilgrim way
    R: we know that you are beside us,
          guiding our steps on the path of peace.

Let the fire of enthusiasm be in your heart
Let the wisdom of Scripture be in your mind
Let the joy of the Spirit be in your life
Let the peace of the Son surround you always
Let the love of the Father enfold you to eternity

*Grey-black clouds, seemingly menacing yet full of promise
Life-giving rain, falling as a curtain from the sky
Streams and rivulets run into rivers
    and the rivers flow majestically down to the sea.
See, the gift of God in the water of life*

RESPONSORIAL PSALM: 113:1–3

L: Praise the Lord.
    Praise, O servants of the Lord,
    praise the name of the Lord.

*R: Let the name of the Lord be praised,
    both now and for evermore.*

L: From the rising of the sun to the place where it sets
R: the name of the Lord is to be praised.

READING: Ephesians 3:1–6

MEDITATION

God calls us to be stewards,
    into whose care is committed the word of life,
    the mystery of God's revelation,
    the proclamation of the good news of Christ
        through the inspiration of the Holy Spirit.
What a privilege! What a responsibility!
Now to you who hear these words we say,
    Have you responded to the good news
    and are you ready to share with others
        the secret of God's love in Christ
            available to all people?

'The administration of God's grace.' (3:2)

PRAYERS

Wise and loving God,
    you reveal to your people the mystery of the universe
        and make known to us the secret of your purpose.
    It is from the depth and breadth of your love
        that you redeem all the nations on earth.
    You love your chosen people, the Jews,
        amongst whom Jesus was born;
    you love all Gentile nations,
        calling your people to respond to the shepherd's call.
    Help us to share the open secret
        that you sent Jesus into the world
    to draw to yourself all people through his great sacrifice.

God of seas and oceans,
    we pray for all those whose work
        takes them in boats and ships across wide seas and oceans.

We pray especially for deep-sea divers
   who see hidden beauty beneath the waves
      but also face concealed dangers in the watery deeps.
May they show courage and skill in all they undertake.
May their exploration and discoveries
be for the benefit of the human community
   and carried out with sensitivity
      for all those other species that live in the seas.

We see the trees clothed in the splendour of warm brown,
   of yellow, golden, russet and hectic red.
We see the moorland turned to autumn
   and hear the birds' song as a symphony.
The heat of summer is gone
   but in the muggy warmth the autumn dress is worn by nature.
We give you praise and thanks, God of creation,
   for the autumnal grace of another day.

RESPONSE

   L: When seas rise and thunder threatens
   R: you, Lord God, bring us to a safe haven.

May the song of the nightingale be a blessing to you
May the flight of the dove be a blessing to you
May the song of the lark be a blessing to you
May the great Creator of all living beings bless you now and always

We welcome the dawn, the sun rising glorious to announce a new day
We rejoice in the noonday, the blessing of work and of leisure
We are content at sunset, heralding a welcome time of rest
God of day and night, be with us in our working and sleeping

RESPONSORIAL PSALM: 115:12–15

L: The Lord remembers us and will bless us.
R: He will bless the house of Israel,
        he will bless the house of Aaron,

L: he will bless those who fear the Lord –
R: small and great alike.

L: May the Lord make you increase,
        both you and your children.
R: May you be blessed by the Lord,
        the Maker of heaven and earth.

READING: Ephesians 3:7–10

MEDITATION

There is power in the proclamation of God's good news;
    there is wisdom in God's great plan of salvation.
He takes ordinary people and makes them extraordinary;
he takes the least of his people to achieve the greatest of tasks,
    preaching to all nations the unsearchable riches of Christ.
God has his great purpose for the world;
    there are secrets and mysteries hidden for generations.
Then comes the time to make all things plain.
Now there is a task for the Church,
    to declare the divine purpose of Christ
        to all people, principalities and powers throughout the universe.
Are you ready to be used for such a great and wonderful purpose?

'The unsearchable riches of Christ.' (3:8)

PRAYERS

Lord Jesus,
    you call us to be servants
        and we find in you both inspiration and example
            for you served your disciples and those around you.
    You show us the way of humility
        since you came from heaven to be one of us;
    help us to show humility in our dealing with others
        since all that we can give and do
            is so little compared to your great love.
    You make us a people of great privilege
        since you commit to us the proclamation
            of the good news of salvation to all nations.

May we not take this privilege lightly;
    may we find fulfilment in doing your will.

Lord of the Dance,
    we give you thanks that you came alongside us on earth
        and that you expressed humour and laughter
            in your dealings with people.
    Give the grace and guidance of your Holy Spirit
        to those who entertain us in our society.
    We pray for clowns
        who bring colour and joyful movement amongst us;
    we pray for puppeteers
        whose work brings happiness to so many children.
    We rejoice that there is something of the child
        in all of us, however old or young.
    We pray that we may be fools for you,
        proclaiming the joyful gospel of your love
            and bringing happiness into many lives.

You are my Shepherd, you lead me when the way is difficult,
    when there are many paths and turnings.
You find me when I have gone astray
    and encourage me to return.
You take me to safe pastures
    when I am reluctant to leave a dangerous place.
You are my Shepherd; you stay with me through the long journey
    and you bring me home.

RESPONSE

    L: Creator God, when we look around
        at the varied colours of your bountiful creation,
        when we hear the myriad sounds of all your creatures,
    R: we praise your name and gladly join in their song of adoration.

May the scent of the rose be a blessing to you
May the sound of the bees be a blessing to you
May the sight of the swallows be a blessing to you
May the voice of God, Father, Son and Spirit, be a blessing to you

DAY 71

Cry of birds, calling high on the mountain
Sound of sea creatures, deep in the ocean
Lowing of cattle, out in the fields
Sound of God's voice, calling to heart and mind

RESPONSORIAL PSALM: 116:5–7

L: The Lord is gracious and righteous;
R: our God is full of compassion.

L: The Lord protects the simple-hearted;
R: when I was in great need, he saved me.

L: Be at rest once more, O my soul,
R: for the Lord has been good to you.

READING: Ephesians 3:11–13

MEDITATION

We can come boldly into God's presence; yet in our selves we pause with awe before the holiness of God. Can we dare to come into his majestic presence?

Yes, because our boldness is based on Christ, our Saviour and our Mediator. He announces us as his friends.

This did not come about by accident. God in his great wisdom and love had his plan to rescue us when we went astray. We are not a people without hope. We put our trust in Christ who suffered for us and we are ready in our turn to suffer for him. To God be the glory for he accomplishes great things for us.

'In him and through faith in him we may approach God with freedom and confidence.' (3:12)

PRAYERS

We come before you, holy God, with confidence;
    not that we are confident in ourselves
but we are made bold through Jesus Christ
    who is our Mediator and Advocate.
By his sacrifice we are saved;
    in his service we have joy;
    in his presence we find peace.
So we offer you our praise
    and we make our requests through Jesus, our Lord and Saviour.

Holy Jesus,
    you founded your church to give glory to your Father.
Guide and inspire all those whom you call
    to positions of leadership in the church.
May they be men and women of vision and faith,
    ready to adventure in discipleship,
    swift to recognise spiritual gifts in others,
    giving a good example in holiness and spirituality,

148

speaking your word with courage.
May they and all the members of your church
  seek to be servants of all for your sake
  and be active in proclaiming the gospel
    for the honour and glory of our Father in heaven.

High lark, bird of the bright song, sing for me.
Swift gazelle, running fast on the wide plain, run for me.
Bright salmon, fish of the upper river, leap for me.
The birds of the air, the beasts of the field,
  the fish of the rivers, are a song of praise
    to the great Lord of sky and sea
      whose dying and rising Son died and rose for me.

RESPONSE

L: Lord God, when your people faithfully proclaim your gospel
      so that others turn to you and find life
*R: there is joy in heaven
      and happiness for your people here on earth.*

*May the God who divided day from night bless you
May the God who said 'Let there be light' bless you
May the God who divided land from water bless you
May the Creator of the heavens and earth bless you now and always*

In the beginning of time I find God
In the end of time I find God
Beyond the reach of time I find God
In the immensity of eternity I know God

RESPONSORIAL PSALM: 118:19–24

L: Open for me the gates of righteousness;
R: I will enter and give thanks to the Lord.

L: This is the gate of the Lord
   through which the righteous may enter.
R: I will give you thanks, for you answered me;
   you have become my salvation.

L: The stone the builders rejected
   has become the capstone;
R: the Lord has done this,
   and it is marvellous in our eyes.

L: This is the day the Lord has made;
R: let us rejoice and be glad in it.

READING: Ephesians 3:14–19

MEDITATION

All families have their foundation in our heavenly Father by whom
they were created. What shall we pray for each family, for each person,
yes, for you too?
   We pray that through his Holy Spirit God may sustain and
      strengthen you in your inner being;
   that by your faith Christ may abide in you;
   that you should be deeply rooted and firmly grounded in love
   that you may understand all things in the height and depth,
      breadth and length.
   And beyond understanding, beyond knowledge
      may you know Christ's love
      and be filled to overflowing with the fullness of God himself.

'Rooted and established in love.' (3:17)

PRAYERS

Father,
   we bow our heads in adoration
      and pray that you will be with us, our family and friends,
         guiding us in our service and witness to you.
Jesus,
   we know that your love for us is deeper than oceans;
      your love for us surpasses knowledge;
   dwell in us and help us to abide in you
      so that we may return your love in full measure.

Holy Spirit,
    strengthen us with your power;
    be within us and around us
        that we may be rooted and grounded in love
           and enabled to live to your glory.
Blessed Trinity,
    fill us with the measure of your fullness
        that we may live in you and you in us.

Healing Spirit,
    we pray for all who face pain and illness,
        especially for those suffering brain damage or deterioration
        whose lives are so limited by their affliction,
        who have glimpses of a happier past,
        who face a bleak future.
Be with the relatives and friends
        who surround them with loving care.
Guide the surgeons, doctors and nurses
        who seek to relieve their suffering and to encourage healing.
Be present that we may see signs and wonders
        in the miracles of grace
    when such people are enabled to face the future
        with faith and courage in spite of their suffering
           or when they experience healing through your power.

Lord,
    you are my coach;
        you see my weak points and you appreciate my strengths.
You are my coach;
        you encourage me to try new techniques and to improve my play.
You are my coach;
        you comfort me when I fail and urge me on towards success.
You are my coach, enabing me to go forward,
    to overcome injury and disappointment.
You are my coach,
    with whose help I win the prize.

RESPONSE

    L: When we go through times of testing
          and all seems dark around us and hope is dimmed
   R: lead us through the darkness to the light beyond
         and renew in us the hope that comes from Christ.

May God, maker of the great creatures, walk with you
May God, maker of the small creatures, go with you
May God, maker of the sea creatures, speak with you
May God, maker of the birds of the air, hear your prayers
May the God of all living creatures bless you now and always

DAY 73

You are the ground of my being, the heart of my love
You are the hope of my planning, the centre of my life
You are the dove of my peace, the core of my confidence
You are my love, my life, my Saviour and my God

RESPONSORIAL PSALM: 121:1–2, 5–8

L: I lift up my eyes to the hills –
  where does my help come from?
R: *My help comes from the Lord,*
  the Maker of heaven and earth.

L: The Lord watches over you –
  the Lord is your shade at your right hand;
R: *the sun will not harm you by day,*
  nor the moon by night.

L: The Lord will keep you from all harm –
  he will watch over your life;
R: *the Lord will watch over your coming and going*
  both now and for evermore.

READING: Ephesians 3:20–21

MEDITATION

There are tasks to be done beyond our imagining;
  there is a mystery to share which is beyond our wisdom.
Yet nothing is too great for us to accomplish
  because God is at work in us and through us
    to work out his mighty purposes.
He uses the church for his great glory
  and so it becomes an instrument of his will.
Belonging to this church, the fellowship of saints,
  you are filled with a power that enables you
    to be and to do far more than you ever dared to hope.
As you too become a channel of God's grace,
  glory is given to Christ your Lord.

'According to his power that is at work within us.' (3:20)

PRAYERS

Merciful God,
  forgive us
    that so often we live as though you lacked power.
  Our concept of you is too small, too limited.
  Our plans are too circumscribed.
  Inspire us to ask in faith
    and give us the assurance
  to know that you will respond
    by doing immeasurably more than we ask or can ever imagine.

152

Let us go forward confidently
   so that your church may glorify your name
   through Jesus Christ our Saviour.

God of freedom,
   we pray for the nation of Taiwan.
   Where there has been persecution, may there be toleration;
   where there has been suspicion and hostility,
      may there be trust and friendship;
   where there has been nationalism and division,
      may there be co-operation and friendship;
   where there has been violence and wounding
      may there be peace and healing.
   May this beautiful island
      be a place of justice and harmony for all its people.

Dear Spirit,
   you are my midwife;
   you make possible the birth of my inner self;
   you encourage me to be born again;
   you enable me to risk new experiences,
      leaving the comfort of the known
      for the adventure of the unknown.
   You are my midwife;
      by your help I am twice-born.

THE LORD'S PRAYER

RESPONSE
   L: Lord, though we may pass through the valley of shadows
         and journey through the gate of suffering
   *R: you bring us to the hilltops of sunlight
         and lead us through the door of healing.*

*May the mystery of the Three surround you
   when you rest in the shade of the tree
   when you climb to the mountain's crest
   when you swim in the ocean's depths
May the mystery of the Three surround you*

To be with you, precious Redeemer, is like the taste of sweetest honey
To taste you is like the choicest of fine wine
To drink of you refreshment as from cool clear water
A taste beyond description, truly divine

RESPONSORIAL PSALM: 122:1–2, 6–9

L: I rejoiced with those who said to me,
      'Let us go to the house of the Lord.'
R: Our feet are standing in your gates, O Jerusalem.

L: Pray for the peace of Jerusalem:
      'May those who love you be secure.
R: May there be peace within your walls
      and security within your citadels.'

L: For the sake of my brothers and friends,
      I will say, 'Peace be within you.'
R: For the sake of the house of the Lord our God,
      I will seek your prosperity.

READING: Ephesians 4:1–6

MEDITATION

What is the life to which you have been called,
   you who take the name of Christ,
      claiming the nature of Christ?
You are called to show humility,
   being patient with those who hurt you,
   being loving towards those who hate you,
   seeking unity with those who put up barriers against you,
   belonging to a fellowship that is united in the Spirit.
You were baptised, as child or believer,
   yet there is one baptism;
you demonstrate spiritual gifts in Quaker quiet or Pentecostal fire,
   yet there is one Spirit;
you are ministers in churches, Catholic, Orthodox or Reformed,
   yet there is one Lord who calls you;
you are members in churches showing and sharing in a variety of gifts
   yet there is one God the Father of all of us,
      whom all are called to worship.

'The unity of the Spirit.' (4:3)

PRAYERS

Lord God and Father of us all,
      help us to show the fruit of your Spirit
         in lives offered for your service.
   Lead us in the way of humility and gentleness,
      finding our example in Jesus.

Give us his patience, even in times of suffering;
  help us to show love to one another
    with sensitivity and understanding
  and may we show in our life together
    the unity which you alone can give.

Companion of the long road,
  we pray for all those who live rough,
  for those who tramp the country lanes and walk the city streets.
  May they receive the gift of food
    when hunger drives them to the stranger's door.
  May they receive the gift of friendship
    when they seek a lift along the hard road.
  May they know your presence
    in the freedom and the danger of a wandering life.

Lord,
  working for the good of all, you are creator;
  walking for the common welfare, you are pilgrim;
  weakened for the world's salvation, you are redeemer;
  whispering to our inner self, you are lover.
Jesus,
  lover of my soul, walk with me to life's end.

RESPONSE

  L: Christ of the upper room,
         may we meet you in welcoming the stranger at our door.
  R: Christ of the open road,
         may we recognise you in the companion we find on our pilgrim way.

As the rain falls from heaven on the hills
As the streams run down to join the river
As the rivers flow down to join the sea
So may you find blessing in communion with God

The darkness when the light of sun and moon is withdrawn
Darkness when not even the glimmer of stars brightens the sky
Darkness when standing alone you can see nothing
Yet God is there in the darkness too;
*   with him the night is as bright as day*

RESPONSORIAL PSALM: 126:1–3

L: When the Lord brought back the captives to Zion,
         we were like men who dreamed.
R: Our mouths were filled with laughter,
*   our tongues with songs of joy.*

L: Then it was said among the nations,
         'The Lord has done great things for them.'
R: The Lord has done great things for us,
*   and we are filled with joy.*

READING: Ephesians 4:7–13

MEDITATION

You are the recipients of the gifts of God,
   called to exercise a ministry in a needy world.
Some are called to be apostles,
   sent out with good news with a care for the churches.
Some are called to be prophets
   speaking the word of the Lord against the injustice of our time,
   warning of the paths that lead to destruction
   and urging people into the way of peace.
Some are called to be evangelists
   proclaiming the good news of God's love in Christ,
   calling people to commitment and discipleship.
Some are called to be pastors
   caring for people in the church and the community,
   offering comfort, help and prayer.
Some are called to be teachers,
   giving instruction in the faith,
   training children, church officials and students for the ministry.
All are concerned with the equipment of the faithful in the task of ministry
   that we may all be more effective channels of peace
      and ambassadors of the gospel,
         united in our faith and mature in our discipleship.

'To prepare God's people for works of service.' (4:12)

PRAYERS

Holy God,
   we confess that we have been content with childlike faith
      when you have been calling us to mature discipleship;
   we have been content with a little spiritual learning

when you desire us to attain the whole measure
of the fullness we find in Christ.
Let us respond to your call with confidence;
some as prophets, courageously to speak your word;
some to be evangelists, joyfully to announce good news;
some to be pastors, lovingly to care for your people;
some to be teachers, wisely to instruct young and old.
So may your people be prepared for your service
through Jesus Christ our Lord.

Divine Spirit,
we pray for all those whose work
faces them with danger on behalf of the community.
We ask for your guidance and protection
for the men and women of the fire service.
May they carry out their tasks with skill,
facing danger with courage,
rescuing people from hazardous situations,
offering their energy and skill
for the service of others.
May we in thankfulness for their dedication
take especial care not to cause fires
and seek to respect the environment
in which we live and see so many of your gifts.

Dear Jesus,
we give you thanks for Andrew
who gladly heard the teaching
that you are the Lamb of God
who takes away the sin of the world.
We give you thanks for Andrew
who took the news to his brother,
proclaiming with joy that he had found the Messiah.
May we be inspired by his example
to take with us everywhere we go
the good news that we have met with the Christ
and that you are the expression of the heart of love,
that in you we shall find our peace.

RESPONSE

L: Holy Redeemer, in thankfulness for all the gifts of creation,
in gratitude for all your gifts of grace,
*R: inspire us to care for our planet earth
and enable us to proclaim the good news of salvation.*

*As the candle burns bright in a dark cave
As the stars cast light on dark streets
As the sun by its dawning scatters the darkness
So may the light of God illumine your life*

Where the breeze blows softly over spring flowers
Where the wind blows strongly over marsh reeds
Where the gale sweeps fiercely over swaying trees
Know that the God of wind and wave speaks to his people.

RESPONSORIAL PSALM: 126:4–6

> L: Restore our fortunes, O Lord,
>   like streams in the Negev.
> *R: Those who sow in tears*
>   *will reap with songs of joy.*
>
> L: He who goes out weeping,
>   carrying seed to sow,
> *R: will return with songs of joy,*
>   *carrying sheaves with him.*

READING: Ephesians 4:14–16

MEDITATION

> Are you like a wisp of straw,
>   carried this way and that by every puff of wind?
> Or are you like a growing plant,
>   firmly rooted in the ground,
>   able to withstand harsh winds
>   and growing ever upwards towards God?
> To use another image,
>   you are part of a body
>   which finds its strength and direction
>   from Jesus Christ, the head.
> This body grows and becomes strong through love.
> So we are within a fellowship,
>   always ready to speak the truth, yet doing so with love,
>   that our unity may be maintained
>   and the body continue to grow.
> Is this the nature of the fellowship to which you belong?
> Is Christ truly the head of the body?
> Is there a caring unity for the good of all?

'Speaking the truth in love.' (4:15)

PRAYERS

> Living God,
>   there are times when we do not speak the truth;
>   for fear or to hurt we tell lies; forgive us.
>   There are times when we speak the truth
>   but in hostility or hate intending to harm; forgive us.
>   Inspire us to speak the truth in love
>   in order to encourage, to guide, to help.

So, growing together in Christ, may we, your people,
    be united with a common mind for a common task.

God of all nations,
    we pray for the nation of Germany.
    Where there has been division, may there be unity;
    where wrong has been inflicted, may there be forgiveness;
    where there has been hurt, may there be healing.
    May the darkness of past deeds
        be scattered by the light of new resolutions.
    May love, patience and compassion
        be expressed by all to all
            so that Germany may be within a family of nations
                committed to peace and justice
                    and the care of our common homeland, earth.

Lord of the Dance,
    we find delight in recalling your celebration
        with the people of Cana in Galilee at a family wedding.
    You joined in the laughter and the dancing;
        you changed the water into wine,
            so preserving the honour of the family
                and the festivity of the occasion.
    Your offer of eternal life is to all
        and there is joy in heaven when people respond.
    May we delight in proclaiming the gospel,
        not with harsh judgement and condemnation
            but in joyful celebration of your love for all people.

RESPONSE
    L: Loving Shepherd, where there is darkness, help us to shed your light;
    R: where there is despair, help us to share your hope.

May the Father bless you with wisdom in your words
May the Son bless you with compassion in your actions
May the Spirit bless you with joy in your service
May God, Father, Son and Spirit, bless you now and always

DAY 77

The seed is in the earth, surrounded by warmth and food
The seed grows secretly, day by day
The seed grows purposefully, ready to break through the soil
May the secret seed of your love ever grow within me

RESPONSORIAL PSALM: 127:1–2

L: Unless the Lord builds the house,
      its builders labour in vain.
R: Unless the Lord watches over the city,
      the watchmen stand guard in vain.

L: In vain you rise early and stay up late,
R: toiling for food to eat –
      for he grants sleep to those he loves.

READING: Ephesians 4:17–24

MEDITATION

Let us be honest with ourselves;
    we show something of the old nature.
Let us bring this before God –
    are we callous, or greedy, or lacking in self-control?
    do we give free rein to passion or deceit?
Let God in his power and love release us.
Bring all that enslaves you before our Father
    that he may forgive and release you.
Then seek God's help
    to put on the new nature,
    to be all that God intended for you,
    to be holy and righteous in your being and living.

'Put on the new self.' (4:24)

PRAYERS

Lord God,
    you are holy and righteous in all your ways
        and you created your people to be like you.
    Forgive us that we fall short of your divine purpose;
        forgive us that in our old self we are children of darkness.
    Help us to put on the new nature;
        since we follow Jesus let us find our inspiration in him,
            and live as children of light.
    Having received the Holy Spirit
        let us show the fruit of the Spirit
            in kindness, goodness and self-control.
    So may we live to your glory
        through Jesus Christ your Son.

Jesus,
    when you began your ministry on earth
        you called a group of young men to be your disciples
            and you trained them to proclaim your gospel.
    We ask for your guidance and inspiration for all youth workers.
    May they be women and men of faith
        who care deeply about the young people in their care.
    In a world of so many evil influences and dangers
        may they be an influence for good.
    By their words and actions
        may they teach young people honesty, integrity
            and the way of service within the community.
    Inspire them with imagination and creativity
        in sharing the good news of your love
        so that they may gently lead many young people to living faith.

Lord,
    you set before me the scales of love.
    What shall I give you, poor as I am?
        I put in the scales my camera with its automatic focus;
        I add in the scales my colour television and video recorder.
    You put in the scales a rough wooden cross
        and the scales are tipped by it.
    What shall I give you, poor as I am?

RESPONSE

    L: Lord, when evil forces pull us in the direction of darkness,
           when temptation draws us into selfish and destructive paths
    R: *may your Holy Spirit lead us in the way of selfless service*
           and powerfully draw us into the light of your presence.

May the Father inspire you with the gift of love
May the Son enliven you with the gift of joy
May the Spirit enfold you with the gift of peace
May God, Father, Son and Spirit, abide with you always

DAY 78

I close my lips and silent hear your word
I close my eyes and blind I see your face
I close my hands and turn to you in prayer
I open my palms and receive your benediction

RESPONSORIAL PSALM: 128:1–2, 5–6

L: Blessed are all who fear the Lord,
     who walk in his ways.
R: You will eat the fruit of your labour;
     blessings and prosperity will be yours.

L: May the Lord bless you from Zion
     all the days of your life;
R: may you see the prosperity of Jerusalem,
     and may you live to see your children's children.
     Peace be upon Israel.

READING: Ephesians 4:25–32

MEDITATION

We know those things which warp our lives and grieve God;
     can we rid ourselves of them?
There is a time to undertake a spiritual audit.
Here on this side are those things which I must reject –
     lies, anger, stealing, dishonesty, evil talk, bitterness,
     slander, malice, or whatever is my particular weakness or
     addiction.
     Here on this side are the things I must affirm –
     truth, kindness, compassion, forgiveness
     and all those qualities which are part of my nature
     as God intended me to be.
Rejecting and affirming is a pattern of life;
     it is an ongoing struggle or a continuing pilgrimage.
If we put our trust in God
     we shall be led by the Spirit in the path of redemption.

'Do not grieve the Holy Spirit of God.' (4:30)

PRAYERS

Holy Spirit,
     at the ending of each day I seek to commune with you
          and I look back at the day and its events.
     There are times when I have caused resentment
          or when I have been made angry by others.
     May the sun not go down with that resentment still present
          or that anger still burning within me.
     Help me to offer and be ready to receive forgiveness.
     Let me not grieve you by what I am or say or do;
          rather let me show your gentleness and love to all.

Holy Spirit,
  inspire, lead and guide me.

Lord of the Universe,
  we give you thanks for all those
    whose inventiveness makes life easier for those around them.
  We pray for inventors and engineers.
  May their skill be made available for the common good.
  May all that they produce be for creative use,
    not for destruction and power seeking.
  May their imagination and dexterity prove a blessing
    for the handicapped, the disabled and the poor.
  May they recognise their skill as a gift from you
    and so offer their inventions and engineering
      not simply for profit but for mutual benefit in society
        and for the glory of your name.

Divine Saviour,
  we give you thanks for the witness of John the Baptist
    who was content to be the forerunner
      announcing your coming to a waiting world.
  We give thanks for his gift in preaching and his humility;
    he was given a task and carried it out with courage;
      then he was ready to decrease even as you increased.
  Inspired by his example may we be eager for work in your kingdom
    yet willing to be laid aside when tasks are complete.
  May we be ready for great tasks or small tasks;
    willing to be in the limelight or in the shadows.
  May we be prepared to do whatever is your will
    and give you the glory, for you are Lord of all.

RESPONSE
  L: Jesus, when there is some great work to be done for you,
        let us not be too afraid to undertake it.
  *R: When there is some small task to be done in your name,
        let us not be too proud to accept it.*

  *May the Father grant you the gift of patience
  May the Son grant you the gift of kindness
  May the Spirit grant you the gift of goodness
  May God, Father, Son and Spirit, bless you day by day*

As the blossom to the fruit
As the seed to the flower
As the acorn to the oak tree
So is my Lord's calling to my discipleship

RESPONSORIAL PSALM: 130:1–2, 5–7

L: Out of the depths I cry to you, O Lord;
    O Lord, hear my voice.

R: *Let your ears be attentive*
    to my cry for mercy.

L: I wait for the Lord, my soul waits,
    and in his word I put my hope.

R: *My soul waits for the Lord*
    more than watchmen wait for the morning,
    more than watchmen wait for the morning.

L: O Israel, put your hope in the Lord,
R: *for with the Lord is unfailing love*
    and with him is full redemption.

READING: Ephesians 5:1–5

MEDITATION

On whom do you model your life? Do you emulate anyone you find to be particularly inspiring? Surely nothing could be more challenging than seeking to imitate God. To do so, we must make our touchstone love, for love is the expression of God's being. Love is at the heart of Christ's sacrifice. Love is the giving of ourselves for others. Love is the proper response of people to God.

Christ has shown us this way for he gave himself as a sacrifice gladly offered; this is the way of giving up one's life for the sake of others, a loss which becomes a gain, a gift which is pleasing to God. This is the way of love, a way to be followed, a life to be emulated.

If this is the way to affirm God's presence we confess that we often reject God by living selfishly, expressing immorality and impurity, thus breaking our relationship with him. Our words, our thoughts, our actions should be those of the saints, holy people. Do we want to belong to the saints or the sinners? Or do we perhaps realise that we are sometimes one, sometimes the other? Our way of life reveals our choice; choose self-indulgence or self-sacrifice. Know clearly that your choice has vital implications. No one can choose the way of darkness and enter the kingdom of God. To be alongside Christ in eternity we must choose to be alongside Christ in time.

'A fragrant offering and sacrifice to God.' (5:2)

PRAYERS

Lord Jesus,
    your love for us is deep and wonderful;
        you offered yourself as a sacrifice on behalf of all of us,
            a fragrant offering.

There was and is no limit to your love.
How can we see such love and fail to respond to it?
How can we go on hurting you by impurity and greed?
Help us to live the life of love,
 being ready to give as you gave,
  offering ourselves joyfully to God our Father.

Laughing Jesus,
 you drew the children around you
  with the magnetism of a clown or pied piper.
Your love for children was evident throughout your ministry.
We pray for children suffering from mental handicap,
 being cared for in their homes or in institutions.
May they know your presence and your love
 and respond to your laughter with smiles.
Inspire and encourage all who care for them,
 their parents, relatives, friends and medical staff,
that their love may be an expression of your love.
So may the children find joy in your presence
  and in the company of those around them
  and overcome their handicap
   by the fullness of the life you give.

Lord Jesus Christ,
 we give you thanks for your encouragement
  to the woman of Samaria who drew water from the well for you.
She received the great gift
 when you spoke to her of the water of eternal life.
We too need your teaching and your encouragement.
Guide us to come to that spring of water
 drinking from which we shall not thirst again,
 receiving which we shall find eternal life,
 refreshed by which we shall walk in your way
  and worship God our Father in spirit and in truth.

RESPONSE

L: Holy Spirit, when we are tempted to hurt others by our words,
   when we are tempted to betray you by our actions,
R: make us open to your gift of power
  and enable us to show your fruit in love.

May the Father bless you with the gift of faithfulness
May the Son inspire in you the quality of gentleness
May the Spirit enable you to exercise self-control
May God, Father, Son and Spirit, bless you this day and always

DAY 80

White riders of the dashing foam
Yellow waves of the swaying corn
Racing greys of the cloudy sky
Heralds of the great God of all creation

RESPONSORIAL PSALM: 131

L: My heart is not proud, O Lord,
      my eyes are not haughty;
R: *I do not concern myself with great matters*
      or things too wonderful for me.

L: But I have stilled and quieted my soul;
R: *like a weaned child with its mother,*
      like a weaned child is my soul within me.

L: O Israel, put your hope in the Lord
R: *both now and for evermore.*

READING: Ephesians 5:6–14

MEDITATION

There are those who choose the way of darkness and prefer to speak and act as children of darkness. But if you follow Jesus you have chosen light; by his inspiration you are light. So be pilgrims of the light. Light is found in the pure and holy, the good and true. Light shows up the ways of darkness for what they are. But you are light.

Light beautifies and clarifies. Light reveals the way. Light enables life. Light expresses God. Light shows us the way to each other. Light is purity. Jesus is the light, gives light and enables his disciples to be light. Choose then to be children of light and in the light experience the glory of the presence of God.

'Now you are light in the Lord.' (5:8)

PRAYERS

Holy God,
      forgive us for those times when we have chosen darkness,
            when we have allowed our minds to dwell on unwholesome thoughts,
            when we have spoken sharp and vindictive words,
            when we have indulged in selfish and unhealthy actions.
      Forgive us for seeking the dark recesses of the mind,
            the deep shadows of pride and passion,
            the murky environment of envy, lust or greed.
      Lead us into the way of light
            and help us to show the fruit of light
                  in holiness and righteousness
                        for the glory of your name.

God of the pilgrim way,
      in the country which we call home
            we are a family of people.

Some of the family were born here
and some have come from other countries,
but we are one people, one family, your children.
We thank you for our variety.
We pray for those who have recently settled here.
Enrich our lives as we share their culture
and as they learn more of our inheritance.
Be near to comfort any who experience fear
or who feel hostility from some people around them.
Grant us all a deeper understanding of each other.
Lead us in the way of reconciliation.
Let us recognise each other as brothers and sisters,
knowing that in Christ there is neither black nor white,
rich nor poor, Gentile nor Jew,
but we are one people, looking to you, our Father,
and bound together in your Holy Spirit.

Healer Jesus,
we recall with thanksgiving the pool in Jerusalem
where so many diseased and ill people gathered
to seek healing in the waters there.
In your compassion you reached out to a cripple;
by your touch he was healed and able to carry his own stretcher.
Give us faith to know that you heal today;
sometimes you heal through the ministry of doctors and nurses;
sometimes you heal through the prayers of your followers;
sometimes you heal through the hands of your ministers.
It is by your divine touch that we are healed
and we give you praise and thanks
for your love and compassion shown to so many people.

THE LORD'S PRAYER

RESPONSE

L: Jesus, you showed a mother's love
in your desire to draw all people to yourself.
R: Help us to show a sister's care
in our willingness to help those in need
and our eagerness to tell your story.

May God the great Spirit accompany your journeying
May God the Mother of all being watch over your progress
May God the spark of all life ignite your enthusiasm
May the triune God, the great mystery, give you a benediction

DAY 81

What is the Spirit?
Not a wraith, a ghost, without substance or personality.
The Spirit is with us,
*   God amongst us,*
offering his gifts to us,
*   seeking to show his fruit through us.*
The fruit of the Spirit is love, joy, peace,
*   patience, kindness, goodness,*
*   faithfulness, gentleness, self-control*

RESPONSORIAL PSALM: 133

L: How good and pleasant it is
        when brothers live together in unity!
        It is like precious oil poured on the head,
        running down on the beard,

R: *running down on Aaron's beard,*
    down upon the collar of his robes.

L: It is as if the dew of Hermon
        were falling on Mount Zion.

R: *For there the Lord bestows his blessing,*
    even life for evermore.

READING: Ephesians 5:15–20

MEDITATION

The life of the Spirit is spontaneous, free, gracious, powerful. Renewal is sweeping through the church and one of the signs is renewed worship. The people gathered to worship sing in spontaneous harmony, praise God and refresh each other with spiritual songs. The presence of the Spirit is demonstrated with signs and wonders for which the people give thanks to God through Christ.

The church is blessed through the gifts of the Spirit. We must also seek to show the fruit of the Spirit for the life of the Spirit is shown in gentleness, moderation, love and peace.

'Sing and make music in your heart to the Lord.' (5:19)

PRAYERS

Lord,
    it is so easy to fall into foolish ways;
        to drink too much and lose control;
            to give way to anger and speak harsh words.
    Help us to be wise in following your way,
        to show self–control and moderation.
    Fill us with your Spirit
        that we may think purely, speak wisely
            and show goodness and kindness in our actions.
    May there be harmony in our life together
        and music in the offering of our lives to you.

Creator God,
   we pray for all those with a gift in singing;
      for opera and concert singers,
         for those whose popular songs delight so many young people,
         for those who sing in church and community choirs.
   We pray that all of them may delight to sing
      both to entertain others and to give you praise.
   We give especial thanks for those
      whose gift of song is expressed for peace and justice
      or to encourage and help those facing difficulty or despair·
      or to praise your name.
   May we all share with joyfulness
      in singing songs both old and new
         to express our worship and to give you glory.

Loving Jesus,
   you are the bread of life;
      when we come to you we do not go hungry.
   In you we find sufficient for all our needs.
   We ask for your blessing for all those in our world
      who lack material bread, the poor, the deprived, the hungry.
   Inspire your people in many places
         to care and to share,
         to give seed and tools
      that the needy may be enabled to help themselves.
   So may we give to all the bread of the world
      and also proclaim you as the bread of life.

RESPONSE
   L: Holy God, as the lark sings your praise in the morning,
         as the dove coos for peace at noonday,
         as the owl hoots its call at night,
   *R: so may we praise you as we rise up in the morning,
         express our gratitude to you by our work throughout the day,
         and gladly voice our thankfulness to you as evening falls.*

   The God of yesterday has done great things for you
   The God of today shows great signs for you
   The God of tomorrow will perform great wonders for you
   The God of eternity, Father, Son and Spirit, bless you now and always

<table>
<tr>
<td>

DAY
82

</td>
<td>

What is love?
  an offering of money on a plate? No.
  an offering of water in a cup? No.
  an offering of wine at table? No.
Love is the offering of myself to God
  who first loved me.
Love is.
Love

</td>
</tr>
</table>

RESPONSORIAL PSALM: 134

  L: Praise the Lord, all you servants of the Lord
  R: who minister by night in the house of the Lord.

  L: Lift up your hands in the sanctuary and praise the Lord.
  R: May the Lord, the Maker of heaven and earth, bless you from Zion.

READING: Ephesians 5:21–32

MEDITATION

Good relationships depend on mutuality; or if we talk of being subject it is to each other, for each other and ultimately for love of Christ. Let us take the attitude of wife and husband. Paul seeks to liken this marriage relationship to the spiritual relationship of Christ and his church. Christ is the head of the church and its Saviour, so the church is subject to Christ.

Is the husband saviour of his wife and family? No, but Paul sees the husband as head of the family and therefore the wife as owing obedience to her husband. Clearly Paul sees this against the social background of his time and to that extent overstates the case in terms of today's world. But the kernel truth is there; the marriage relationship is a spiritual one as well as a physical one. The husband has certain responsibilities and the wife hers. If obedience is promised, it can be so in a context of love.

The relationship of love is mutual. In some ways within marriage the relationship of obedience is mutual too, for Paul says 'Be subject to one another'. In another way Paul distinguishes roles more clearly in marriage than could easily be done today. The heart of the matter remains love and trust. When love and trust are absent in a marriage it has fallen apart; when they are present it can withstand great trials. In a spiritual marriage, such love is more than romantic attraction; it continues through the years.

'Wives, submit to your husbands, as to the Lord.
. . . Husbands, love your wives, just as Christ loved the church.' (5:22, 25)

PRAYERS

Loving Father,
  we thank you for the joy of family life,
    especially for the love that binds wife and husband.
  We thank you for the faith of Abraham and Sarah,
    of Isaac and Rebekah, and others who in distant times
      took the way of pilgrimage in response to your word.

We thank you for Mary and Joseph
    who gave a family home to Jesus.
We thank you for Priscilla and Aquila and other saintly people
    who offered their homes and their lives
        for the work of your kingdom.
May husbands and wives today show such faith and love
    in the work of your kingdom and the service of others.

Holy Spirit,
    we ask for your guidance and inspiration for all community workers.
    As they work alongside the deprived,
        as they engage in community action
            and encourage others in service and common care,
        as they organise clubs and serve on committees,
    may they show skill, understanding and compassion.
    We pray for church-related community workers
        that by their words and example
            they may inspire action together for the common good
                and be signs of the kingdom in a world of need.

Lord Jesus,
    you are the light of the world;
    those who follow you do not walk in darkness
        but have the light of life.
We hold before you the people who live in darkness,
    who experience despair or pass through times of depression.
Help us to offer friendship which brings light;
    inspire us to speak of hope which scatters the darkness.
May your people everywhere be a source of light
    and proclaim to all that you are the light of the world.

RESPONSE

    L: Living Redeemer, may women and men follow in your way,
           may black and white worship you in unison.
    R: May young and old join to praise you,
          may every generation delight to walk the pilgrim path.

    May you find deep stillness in your ocean journey
    May you find deep quiet on the high mountain
    May you find the inward silence of mystic contemplation
    May the peace of the blessed Trinity be yours to your life's fulfilment

DAY 83

What is joy?
a frothy spice of laughter? No.
an exuberant dance of gaiety? No.
a flamboyant shout of praise? No.
Joy is deep and true and strong.
Joy is found in believing, lost in God.
Joy is.
Joy

RESPONSORIAL PSALM: 138:4–5, 8

L: May all the kings of the earth praise you, O Lord,
         when they hear the words of your mouth.
R: May they sing of the ways of the Lord,
*   for the glory of the Lord is great.*

L: The Lord will fulfil his purpose for me;
R: your love, O Lord, endures for ever –
*   do not abandon the works of your hands.*

READING: Ephesians 6:1–4

MEDITATION

In all of life there has to be mutuality, a rhythm of give and take. This applies too to the relationship between parents and children. The wisdom of age should have something to impart in experience so it is right that children should give obedience to their parents. Parents in their turn owe something to their children; discipline which is firm yet understanding, clear but given in love. And with it should go, by word and example, teaching in the faith.

In this context we should remember that the church is a family too. Adults give parental guidance and help whether parents or not. Children know themselves part of a wider family, a community of love, looking to God the Father of all of us. In such a family all are children with something to learn; all become parents with much to give; all receive and give in a mutual process of learning and discipleship.

'Children, obey your parents in the Lord.' (6:1)

PRAYERS

Loving Redeemer,
       we give you thanks for childhood blessings.
   As you found joy in the earthly home at Nazareth
       so we recall our own home life,
           the love of parents and happiness of the family.
   We give you thanks too for our place of work
       and the web of relationships that binds us together.
   We thank you that in society
       all have something to give and something to receive.
   Help us to know that in Christ
       we enter into a wider family

172

and find many brothers and sisters
in all those people who walk in your way.

God of every generation,
we hold before you the elderly of our community:
the housebound, kept home by age or handicap;
the lonely, who miss those who have gone before;
the fearful, who dare not unlock the door;
the doubting, who wonder whether the future is assured;
the despairing, whose experiences have broken their spirit.
We hold before you all those
who have fulfilled a lifetime of service,
who accept age with grace and face the future with faith,
whose self-sacrifice and generosity are an inspiration.
Bless the elderly in our community;
may they be held in honour by us all.

God of peace,
lead us in the way of harmony.
May the leaders of the nations seek peace and justice;
may our country uphold righteousness and concord;
may we seek the welfare of all
in each village, town and city.
Give to each of us health of body, mind and spirit
and may we be at peace with you and with our neighbours.

RESPONSE

L: When the Holy Spirit calls us to adventure in discipleship
R: may we have the courage and faith to respond.

May the God of the changing seasons bless your years
May the God of all living creatures bless your journeys
May the God of sun, moon and stars bless your meditation
May God, Father, Son and Holy Spirit, bless you in discipleship

DAY 84

What is peace?
  a treaty between trading nations? No.
  a quiet time bought at a price? No.
  an iron hand keeping dissidents in check? No.
Peace is the presence of God.
Peace is harmony between neighbours.
Peace is justice twinned with righteousness.
Peace is.
Peace

RESPONSORIAL PSALM: 139:1–4

L: O Lord, you have searched me and you know me.
R: You know when I sit and when I rise;
    you perceive my thoughts from afar.

L: You discern my going out and my lying down;
    you are familiar with all my ways.
R: Before a word is on my tongue
    you know it completely, O Lord.

READING: Ephesians 6:5–9

MEDITATION

If management and union relationships were always governed by mutuality there would be less problems in factories. Employees with Christian commitment should work to the best of their ability not simply to please their employers but in service to Christ. But as for one, so for the other; the employers should be fair and considerate, giving a good reward for work well done.

This makes for a well-ordered society, each contributing to society according to his or her ability, each receiving from society according to his or her need. There should be fair recognition of intellectual and management input but, equally, recognition of input through manual work. All should be valued as making an essential contribution to society and monetary reward should not show high differentials. A contented society arises from co-operative effort. Paul is right in seeing the basis of the social contract in the relationships of people to God.

'*Serve wholeheartedly, as if you were serving the Lord.*' (6:7)

PRAYERS

Carpenter Jesus,
    we pray for all who are involved in the industrial scene;
  for those on the shop floor
    that they may offer their skill for the common good;
  for those who work as supervisors and managers
    that they may show understanding and kindness;
  for directors and shareholders
    that they may not put profit before the interests
      of the whole workforce and the community

174

but rather seek to direct a united operation
for mutual benefit and the common good;
we pray for union officials and members
that they may always have in mind not only their own interests
but the efficiency of the company and the welfare of all.
So may industry flourish for the health of the nation
and as an offering of work to you.

Come down, Holy Spirit, promised gift of Jesus;
come quickly.
Enlarge our minds, uplift our spirits,
open our eyes and ears, sharpen our senses.
Come down, Holy Spirit.
Break us, make us, enliven us, renew us.
Instil your wisdom, power and love in us
that we may be mightily used
in the service of our heavenly Father.

Loving Shepherd,
we give you thanks that you care for your people,
being ready to sacrifice your life for our sakes.
You are the good Shepherd;
you know your sheep by name and care for all individually.
When danger threatens you are there to protect;
when sheep wander away and are lost
you search until you find them
and then return them to the fold.
You care for your sheep whatever the cost
and you draw us together
so we are one flock, one shepherd.

RESPONSE

L: Some put their trust in money and some seek fulfilment in power.
*R: Lord, help us to put our trust in you
and to seek the power that comes from your Holy Spirit.*

*May the God of earthquake, wind and fire inspire you
May the God of the still small voice speak to you
May the God of mystic communion be one with you
May God, Father, Son and Spirit, be with you to your journey's end*

DAY 85

Patience is care of others,
  ready to listen rather than speak.
Patience gives time for people,
  has time for God.
Patience begins but never ends.
Patience understands when people fail.
Patience knows that God never fails

RESPONSORIAL PSALM: 139:17–18, 23–24

L: How precious to me are your thoughts, O God!
R: How vast is the sum of them!

L: Were I to count them,
    they would outnumber the grains of sand.
R: When I awake, I am still with you.

L: Search me, O God, and know my heart;
    test me and know my anxious thoughts.
R: See if there is any offensive way in me,
    and lead me in the way everlasting.

READING: Ephesians 6:10–12

MEDITATION

There is a conflict; it is taking place in our world in our time. This is not a conflict between nations, not a battle between people, although sadly there is all too much human conflict. No, this is a spiritual conflict between powers, against world rulers in darkness, between the hosts of heavenly powers. This is the struggle of light and darkness, of good and evil, and it has a cosmic dimension.

The signs of this are clear in the spiritual sickness of our lives; when people resort to occult practices, using ouija boards, reading tarot cards, dabbling with black magic. This is a time to stand up for truth, to proclaim good news, to declare the trust and righteousness of the living God. For this conflict spiritual armour is needed and such is provided by our God.

'Be strong in the Lord.' (6:10)

PRAYERS

Lord God,
    sustain us in times of spiritual aridity,
    guide us when we have lost our way,
    protect us in times of spiritual conflict,
    renew us when we are in despair;
    lead us to a rock when we are in a spiritual storm,
    give us faith after times of doubt,
    equip us with gifts of the Spirit for the spiritual struggle,
    restore us to health in body, mind and spirit.

Living Spirit,
we pray for the people of Russia and America.
Guide the leaders and people into the ways of peace and freedom,
of mutual understanding, forgiveness and love.
Rejecting the persecution and faults of the past
may they build a new era of peace and righteousness,
of freedom, truth and trust.
We pray especially for the members of the church in these places;
may the denials and failures of the past be forgiven;
may the suffering and martyrdoms of the past be an inspiration;
may the challenge of the future be accepted
in the name of Christ.
May these two great nations lead the way
in seeking the welfare of their own and other peoples
and working for security, justice and peace
throughout the world.

Risen Jesus,
you are the resurrection and the life;
whoever believes in you does not die
but enters into the life that is eternal.
This is the good news we share with all people –
that death does not have dominion over us;
death is not an end but a door to new life.
You have opened for us the gates of life
so we can look forward to perpetual joy.
Inspire us to proclaim that good news
to all who are ready to hear
that they may believe and have eternal life.

RESPONSE

L: God of light, when the struggle is intense and the conflict hard,
when we go through times of testing and storms,
R: guard us, protect us, inspire us
and lead us to the safety of the rock, the place of refuge.

As the sun in its shining brings glory
As the stars in the night scatter dark
As the moon gives us hope in its radiance
So may the light of God
fill your heart and your mind and your life.

DAY 86

Kindness does not count the cost.
Kindness does not beg the question.
Kindness
    offers a way up to those who are down,
    waits for those who have fallen behind,
    gives to those who have nothing on which to survive
    and receives from those who thought they had nothing to give

RESPONSORIAL PSALM: 141:1–2

    L: O Lord, I call to you; come quickly to me.
    R: Hear my voice when I call to you.

    L: May my prayer be set before you like incense;
    R: may the lifting up of my hands be like the evening sacrifice.

READING: Ephesians 6:13–15

MEDITATION

    What are the spiritual weapons with which God equips us? Truth is one of the most powerful. God's truth is made known through his holy Word; it is expressed through the living Word, Jesus. Value truth; avoid the lies that undermine trust. Truth brings freedom; it opens the way to new life. Do not criticise those who search for truth since their search will lead them ultimately to God.

    Another weapon is righteousness. God alone does what is wholly right. But we are to seek what is right too. We are surrounded by people willing to do wrong for ambition, pride or greed. But those who walk the way of righteousness do not count the cost. To defend the right is its own reward. Do not criticise those who stand up for what is right, for they walk the way of God.

    Another piece of armour is the gospel of peace. Peace is good news for it is God's intention for his world. Around us is a world that has resorted too often to war. Yet it is also a matter of aggressive speech and attitude in personal relationships; these too undermine peace. Peace is wholeness, welfare, health. It is the true well-being of all people, all creatures and the creation itself. Peace is God's gift for his people; equipped with peace we are defended against many of life's hazards.

'The readiness that comes from the gospel of peace.' (6:15)

PRAYERS

    Loving Father,
        help us to stand our ground against evil,
            to speak the truth and oppose injustice;
        guide us in rejecting what is wrong and unworthy,
            and choosing the way of righteousness and goodness;
        enable us to renounce violence and war
            and inspire us to announce your message of peace.

Spirit of creativity,
　　we give thanks for all those who add to the joy of life
　　　　by their skills and gifts in cooking and baking.
　　We pray that they may use their skills
　　　　for the health and welfare of all,
　　　　whether in the daily provision of meals
　　　　　　or the special occasions and celebrations.
　　As we give thanks for the fellowship of the table
　　　　we remember the hungry and needy of the world.
　　May we never be so absorbed with satisfying our own needs
　　　　that we forget those who lack food and shelter.
　　As we have been blessed by your provision for us
　　　　so may we be ready to share with others
　　　　　　as a sign of our gratitude to you
　　　　and an expression of the compassion of Jesus Christ our Lord.

Living Lord Jesus,
　　you were ready to pass through death
　　　　that you might offer your people life.
　　You were ready to fall like the grain of wheat into the ground
　　　　that there might be fruit for God's glory.
　　Teach us your way that we too may be ready
　　　　to be like the grain of wheat, hidden in the ground,
　　　　that in the fullness of time we might bear a great crop,
　　　　　　showing fruit for the glory of God our Father.

RESPONSE

　　L:　Lord, when the green shoots push through the hard ground
　　　　　　we know that there is the promise of spring.
　　*R:　When conflict is ended and words of forgiveness are spoken
　　　　　　we know there is the promise of peace.*

　　*May the maker of light give light to your eyes
　　May the restorer of sight give sight to your eyes
　　May the guide of the inward seeing give depth to your eyes
　　May Father, Son and Spirit be in your seeing and your being*

Goodness has no jaundiced eye.
Goodness has no gossip's tongue.
Goodness has no critic's ear.
Goodness
thinks well of others,
looks to the welfare of the nation,
guards the well-being of the planet.
Goodness is good news

RESPONSORIAL PSALM: 142:5–7

L: I cry to you, O Lord;
R: I say, 'You are my refuge,
my portion in the land of the living.'

L: Listen to my cry,
for I am in desperate need;
R: rescue me from those who pursue me,
for they are too strong for me.

L: Set me free from my prison,
that I may praise your name.
R: Then the righteous will gather about me
because of your goodness to me.

READING: Ephesians 6:16–17

MEDITATION

The heavenly armour includes faith. Through faith ancient enmities are overcome; in faith the seemingly impossible becomes possible and great feats are accomplished; faith in God enables us to face overwhelming odds in human terms; faith brings us through a crisis; faith keeps our feet steady on a narrow path we cannot even see. Faith is the bedrock foundation of our life.

And alongside faith, salvation – not earned by us but given by the free grace of God. The culmination of this life, the promise of eternal life, this is salvation brought about by Christ on the cross. Around us are all the threats of destruction, the life-denying spirits of negativity. But in Christ is found our salvation.

In the cosmic conflict we are also equipped with the Spirit, God's enabler of vulnerable and weak disciples. If we moved forward relying on our own strength we would fall on the spiritual battlefield of life. By God's Spirit we find strength in the word of God. By God's Spirit we are led in the way of God. By God's Spirit we become instruments of the will of God. So may our defence be found in God's gift in the Spirit.

'Take the helmet of salvation and the sword of the Spirit.' (6:17)

PRAYERS

Living God,
inspire in us a faith that does not count the cost,
faith that is ready to adventure in discipleship,
faith that responds joyfully to your call.

Make us thankful for our salvation brought about by Christ;
through that salvation may we have full assurance
and in salvation may we have a joy that never ends.

Healing Spirit,
we pray for those suffering from serious diseases
and for those who are terminally ill.
We pray for skill and patience for the doctors and nurses
who care for them in hospitals and hospices.
We pray that their relatives and friends, giving love and care,
may be strengthened and comforted.
May their faith not falter nor their courage fail
as they encourage and support each other through testing times.
We pray for those suffering from AIDS
as they face all the problems of terminal illness
and often the added burden of criticism and misunderstanding.
We pray for guidance for all those engaged in research
that by your inspiration and their skill ways may be found
to overcome the scourges of our present generation.
Help us to live in your way
and to seek your healing in our body, mind and spirit.

Servant Jesus,
you taught us so wonderfully
in your actions as well as your words.
So you took the towel and the basin of water
and washed the dusty feet of your disciples.
May we consider no task too humble,
no job too mean, no office too lowly,
to undertake for your kingdom.
So may we be the servant people
ready at all times to follow and obey our Servant King.

RESPONSE

L: Lord, help us to offer service without counting the cost,
to engage in struggle without complaining about the wound.
*R: Lord, inspire us to work without seeking rewards
and to find our fulfilment in doing your will.*

The maker of the silver fish, cascading shoal, be near you
The maker of the great fish, white whale, be around you
The maker of the gentle fish, playful dolphin, be close to you
May the Great Lord of sea creatures swim with you

DAY
88

Faithfulness is not afraid to take a dangerous road.
Faithfulness stays alongside the one who is down.
Faithfulness knows that God journeys with us.
Faithfulness offers to God time and talents.
Faithfulness trusts God whatever happens

RESPONSORIAL PSALM: 145:3–4, 6–7

L: Great is the Lord and most worthy of praise;
R: his greatness no one can fathom.

L: One generation will commend your works to another;
R: they will tell of your mighty acts.

L: They will tell of the power of your awesome works,
        and I will proclaim your great deeds.
R: They will celebrate your abundant goodness
        and joyfully sing of your righteousness.

READING: Ephesians 6:18–20

MEDITATION

At the heart of the spiritual life is prayer. Sustaining us in the spiritual conflict
is prayer. It is not some rarefied atmosphere reserved for spiritual astronauts.
Rather it is the intimate conversation between people and our God. Prayer unites
us to God; prayer opens the way to the kingdom of heaven; prayer is the release
of our spiritual potential. In prayer we are realised.

So we pray for each other; we pray for the missionaries, the preachers, the
teachers. We pray that doors may open for the gospel to be proclaimed; we pray
for the persecuted church, that the saints may endure whatever the suffering they
face and that the persecution may be ended. May we too count it our greatest
privilege to share the good news of God's love.

'Pray in the Spirit on all occasions.' (6:18)

PRAYERS

Father,
    when we come before you in praise
        our voices and our lives are filled with joy;
    when we come before you in confession
        we know ourselves unworthy to be in your holy presence;
    when we come before you in prayer for others
        we know that you respond in your wisdom and your love;
    when we wait on you in meditation
        we are lifted to the third heaven in mystic communion.
    May your name be praised in time and eternity
        for your forgiveness, your blessings and our union with you
            through Christ our Saviour and Redeemer.

Spirit of beauty,
  we give thanks for those whose creativity and skill
    contribute to the beauty of our surroundings.
  We pray for builders, decorators and landscape gardeners.
  May they count it a privilege
    to give joy to others and glory to your name
      by the work they do in buildings and in grounds.
  We give thanks that we derive so much pleasure
    from living in or visiting houses
      that are beautifully decorated
    and walking through parks or gardens
      that have been laid out with loving care.
  As we see the inspiration for all of this
    in the beauty of nature
  may we seek to be good stewards of all that you have given us
    in the loveliness of planet earth.

Holy Jesus,
  what a wonderful experience you gave to your disciples
    when you shared together in the Passover feast.
  You broke the bread and passed it to your friends;
    you poured the wine and shared it with your disciples.
  In that mystic moment they were made one with you
    and beyond the bounds of time
      your body and your blood united them and you
        with your followers in every generation.
  So may we enter into that mystery;
    each time we receive the bread and wine at communion
      may we know ourselves one with you and all your people.

RESPONSE
  L: Holy God, there are many times when we are conscious of the ordinary
        and the tasks we undertake are prosaic;
  *R: but we give you thanks that there are other occasions
        when we are lifted to the third heaven in mystic communion with you.*

  May your feet walk in the way of the Lord
  May your voice speak the word of the Lord
  May your hands serve God in blessing others
  May your life show something of the glory of God
  May you know the peace of God now and always

DAY 89

Gentleness deals with no one harshly.
Gentleness has no rule book and no penalty.
Gentleness is always ready to forgive.
Gentleness
  leads the way to new hope,
  opens the way to new life
  and finds the way to God

RESPONSORIAL PSALM: 147:1, 3–5

L: Praise the Lord.
  How good it is to sing praises to our God,
R: how pleasant and fitting to praise him!

L: He heals the broken-hearted and binds up their wounds.
R: He determines the number of the stars and calls them each by name.

L: Great is our Lord and mighty in power;
R: his understanding has no limit.

READING: Ephesians 6:21–22

MEDITATION

  Communication is so important – to convey to people what we feel about them, our concern for them. Today there are so many ways of communicating: in crisis, by telegram; at more leisure, by letter; graciously, with flowers; aboard ship, by flags; better than all these is to go ourselves to meet our friends and say all that is to be said; and when that is not possible, then to send a personal messenger who can speak on our behalf.

  Tychicus was a personal messenger from Paul to the Ephesian Christians; sent to give them news of Paul and to encourage them in discipleship. Paul was unable to go since he was a prisoner but his friend would speak eloquently for him.

  We too are sent as messengers by God, to speak for him to many people; to give them news of God's love declared in Christ and to encourage them to be faithful disciples.

'That he may encourage you.' (6:22)

PRAYERS

  Holy God,
    we thank you that you have given us your word,
      speaking to us through the scripture;
    we thank you that you have given us the living Word,
      Jesus who, in obedience to your will,
        lived and taught amongst us and gave his life on the cross
          that we might have forgiveness and eternal life;
    in responding to your love
      we come into the fellowship of the church;
    help us to be faithful to you

184

in sharing the good news with others
of all that you have done for us in Christ our Saviour.

God of justice and righteousness,
we pray for the people of Romania.
In a country of many nationalities,
in a place that holds many bitter memories,
may there be reconciliation expressed in justice
and bearing its fruit in righteousness and peace.
We give thanks that the response to needs in Romania
demonstrated a family of nations, united in concern.
May that response in compassion
result in growing harmony and common action.
May the persecution and suffering endured by your church
be the seed of new growth and deepened faith.
May the people build together for a secure and peaceful future
inspired by your Son, Jesus Christ our Lord.

Crucified Lord,
you teach us by word and example to love one another.
No person can show greater love than by giving his own life.
Such a depth of love was yours for your people
and that love has continued through all generations.
Inspire us to show such love to those we meet
as an expression of your love
and in doing so may we find and share your joy.

RESPONSE

L: Lord, when a waiting world is hungry for the bread of life
*R: give us the inspiration to share with others
the eternal bread of heaven, offered in sacrifice here on earth.*

May the Lord of the silver moon shine upon you
May the King of the myriad stars reign over you
May the Maker of the bright sun shed warmth around you
May the living Centre of the great Universe draw you to himself

DAY 90

Self-control keeps the appetite in check.
Self-control keeps hate and enmity at bay.
Self-control resists passion, jealousy and greed.
Self-control enables me to be true to self
*   and helps me to be true to God.*
Self-control for self-realisation

RESPONSORIAL PSALM: 150

L: Praise the Lord.
       Praise God in his sanctuary;
       praise him in his mighty heavens.
R: *Praise him for his acts of power;*
       praise him for his surpassing greatness.

L: Praise him with the sounding of the trumpet,
       praise him with the harp and lyre,
R: *praise him with tambourine and dancing,*
       praise him with the strings and flute.

L: Praise him with the clash of cymbals,
       praise him with resounding cymbals.
R: *Let everything that has breath praise the Lord.*
       Praise the Lord.

READING: Ephesians 6:23–24

MEDITATION

If we could give to others a benediction what better blessing than peace, love and faith?

Peace – shalom – that inner harmony which is reflected in peace with our neighbours.

Love – the outpouring of ourselves for others, the bringing together of people in self-giving.

Faith – which is on utter trust, reliance on the living God in the sure knowledge that he will keep you wherever you go.

May such peace, such love, such faith, be with you and sustain you in life's pilgrimage, the gift of God our Father and Christ our Saviour.

And that your joy may be complete may Christ grant you grace – his gentleness, his courtesy, his self-offering.

May the grace of Christ bind together all those who love the Lord in sincerity and in truth.

'*Grace to all who love our Lord Jesus Christ with an undying love.*' (6:24)

PRAYERS

Creator God,
   help us to look to Jesus and to find in him
       our inspiration to show the grace of patience and kindness
           in all our dealings with others.

May we find peace in our communion with you
    and work for harmony amongst our neighbours.
May we seek to express love in our life together
    and may we see love transforming the world.
Be with us in our pilgrimage of faith
    that in all our words and works
        we may give honour to you, Father, Son and Holy Spirit,
           one God, for ever.

Life-giving Spirit,
    in every generation you call and equip
        those who are to be ministers of the gospel.
Guide and enable all those called into various ministries today.
As they serve in local churches, in hospitals and colleges,
    may they teach the faith wisely,
    may they preach the gospel faithfully,
    may they celebrate the sacraments joyfully,
    may they serve the needy compassionately,
    may they confront injustice prophetically,
    may they care for their people pastorally.
In all their word and work of ministry
    may they have your gifts and show your fruit
        in the name of Jesus our Saviour.

Risen Lord, the sign of your presence was the gift of peace.
    When your disciples met you
        they received the greeting of peace and were filled with wonder.
Risen Lord, the sign of your presence is the gift of peace.
    When we meet you in worship or on the mountain top
        your words of greeting fill our hearts with peace
           and we joyfully proclaim your name to our generation.
Risen Lord, the sign of your presence will be peace
    when you come again in glory to judge all people
    and to receive your chosen into the joy of your eternal kingdom.

RESPONSE

    L: Holy God, when the darkness of doubt is ended,
        when the winter of despair is gone,
        when the dark night of the soul is completed
    R: we greet with joy the dawn of renewed faith,
        we welcome the spring of new hope,
        we open our hearts to the assurance of the resurrection morning.

May the God of eternity bless you through the years
May the God of time bless you all your days
May the God who is Alpha be with you all your life
May the God who is Omega be with you to your end

Appendix
PRAYERS FOR THE DAY

SUNDAY

Lord, make me an instrument of your peace.
  Where there is hatred, let me sow love;
  where there is injury, pardon;
  where there is doubt, faith;
  where there is despair, hope;
  where there is darkness, light;
  where there is sadness, joy.
O divine Master,
  grant that I may not so much seek
  to be consoled as to console;
  to be understood as to understand;
  to be loved as to love.
  For it is in giving that we receive,
  in pardoning that we are pardoned,
  and in dying that we are born to eternal life.

St Francis of Assisi

MONDAY

Grant, O Lord God,
  that we may cleave to you without parting,
  worship you without wearying,
  serve you without failing,
  faithfully seek you,
  happily find you,
  for ever possess you,
  the only one God, blessed world without end.

St Anselm

TUESDAY

I bind unto myself today,
the strong name of the Trinity,
by invocation of the same,
the Three in One and One in Three.
Christ be with me, Christ within me,
Christ behind me, Christ before me,
Christ beside me, Christ to win me,
Christ to comfort and restore me,
Christ beneath me, Christ above me,
Christ in quiet, Christ in danger,
Christ in mouth of friend and stranger.
Praise to the Lord of my salvation;
salvation is of Christ the Lord.

St Patrick

188

WEDNESDAY

The Light of Peace

We light this candle for peace, Lord.
  May its light scatter the darkness;
  may its flame be a symbol of hope;
  may its burning be a sign of faith
    joining with many other lights for peace.
We light this candle for peace.
  May our lives be an expression of peacemaking;
  may we seek to be lights in a dark world,
  pointing to you, Jesus, the Prince of Peace,
    and following you in the way of peace.
Let the candle burn, as a sign for peace,
    offered to you.

John Johansen-Berg

THURSDAY

O God, you are the light of the minds that know you,
  the life of the souls that love you,
  and the strength of the wills that serve you.
Help us so to know you that we may truly love you,
  so to love you that we may fully serve you,
  whom to serve is perfect freedom;
    through Jesus Christ our Lord.

After St Augustine of Hippo

FRIDAY

O God, the King of righteousness,
  lead us, we pray, in the ways of justice and peace;
  inspire us to break down all oppression and wrong,
  to gain for everyone a due reward,
  and from everyone due service;
  that each may live for all,
  and all may care for each,
  in the name of Jesus Christ our Lord.

After Archbishop William Temple

SATURDAY

O God, you are both the light and the guide
  of them that put their trust in you.
  Grant us in all our doubts and uncertainties,
  the grace to ask what you would have us do;
  that the Spirit of wisdom may save us from all false choices,
  and that in your light we may see light;
  through Jesus Christ our Lord.

William Bright (altered)

Inter-faith Prayer for Peace

Lord, lead me from death to life, from falsehood to truth;
lead me from despair to hope, from fear to trust;
lead me from hate to love, from war to peace.
Let peace fill our heart, our world, our universe.
Peace   peace   peace